FUNDAMENTALS OF
English Grammar

FIFTH EDITION

FUNDAMENTALS OF English Grammar

FIFTH EDITION
WORKBOOK
VOLUME B

Betty S. Azar
Stacy A. Hagen
Geneva Tesh

Fundamentals of English Grammar, Fifth Edition
Workbook Volume B

Copyright © 2020, 2011, 2003, 1992, 1985 by Pearson Education, Inc.
All rights reserved.

No part of this publication may be reproduced, stored in a retrieval system, or transmitted
in any form or by any means, electronic, mechanical, photocopying, recording, or otherwise,
without the prior permission of the publisher.

Pearson Education, 221 River Street, Hoboken, NJ 07030

Azar Associates: Sue Van Etten, Manager

Staff credits: The people who made up the ***Fundamentals of English Grammar, Fifth Edition,***
Workbook team, representing content development, design, project management, publishing,
and rights management, are Pietro Alongi, Sheila Ameri, Warren Fischbach, Sarah Henrich,
Niki Lee, Amy McCormick, Robert Ruvo, Paula Van Ells, and Joseph Vella.

Production Editor: Jennifer McAliney

Text composition: Aptara

Photo Credits: Page 127: Millena/Shutterstock; 140: B Calkins/Shutterstock; 144: Strelka/
Shutterstock; 151: Arvind Singh Negi/Red Reef Design Studio/Pearson India Education Services
Pvt. Ltd.; 159: Puslatronik/Shutterstock; 164: Studio 8/Pearson Education Ltd; 174 (street
signs): James Steidl/Shutterstock; 174 (camping): Oliveromg/Shutterstock; 181: Jackf/123RF; 186
(luggage): Inara Prusakova/Shutterstock; 186 (dishes): Vladimir Rublev/123RF; 187 (x-ray): Ealisa/
Shutterstock; 187 (cast): Stacy Barnett/Shutterstock; 191: AridOcean/Shutterstock; 195 (top right):
Shri Vishishta Chintamani Technologies Private Limited/Pearson India Education Services Pvt. Ltd;
195 (center): Ajisai25/123RF; 196: Goodluz/Shutterstock; 205: Winston Link/Shutterstock; 208 (left):
Germanskydiver/Shutterstock; 208 (right): Danshutter/Shutterstock; 209: WitR/Shutterstock; 220:
Elena Nichizhenova/Shutterstock; 223: Scanrail1/Shutterstock; 226: Bigemrg/123RF; 230: Andrey_
Popov/Shutterstock; 234: East/Shutterstock; 235: Luminaimages/Shutterstock; 237: Lorelyn Medina/
Shutterstock.

Printed in the United States of America

ISBN 10: 0-13-515948-2
ISBN 13: 978-0-13-515948-4

1 2019

Contents

Chapter 10   THE PASSIVE 159

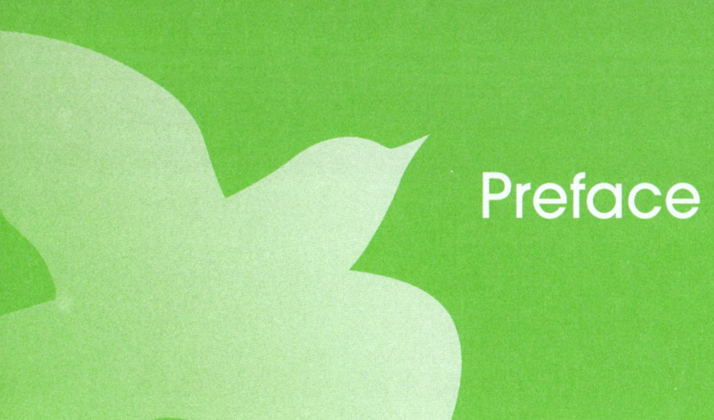

Preface

The *Fundamentals of English Grammar Workbook* is a place for lower-intermediate and intermediate students to explore and practice English grammar on their own. It is a place where they can test and fine-tune their understanding of English structures and improve their ability to use English meaningfully and correctly. All of the exercises have been designed for independent study, but this book is also a resource for teachers who need exercise material for additional classwork, homework, testing, or individualized instruction.

The *Workbook* is keyed to the explanatory grammar charts found in *Fundamentals of English Grammar, Fifth Edition*, a classroom teaching text for English language learners, and in the accompanying *Chartbook*, a grammar reference with no exercises.

The answers to the practices can be found in the *Answer Key* in the back of the *Workbook*. Its pages are perforated so that they can be detached to make a separate booklet. However, if teachers want to use the *Workbook* as a classroom teaching text, the *Answer Key* can be removed at the beginning of the term.

Two special *Workbook* sections called *Phrasal Verbs* and *Preposition Combinations*, not available in the main text, are included in the *Appendices*. These sections provide reference charts and a variety of exercises for independent practice.

CHAPTER 8

Connecting Ideas: Punctuation and Meaning

PRACTICE 1 ▶ Connecting ideas with *and*. (Chart 8-1)

<u>Underline</u> the words that are connected with ***and***. Label these words as nouns, verbs, or adjectives.

                       noun   +   noun

1. The Harbor Hotel combines <u>comfort</u> and <u>style</u>.

              adjective + adjective + adjective

2. Our hotel is <u>beautiful</u>, <u>modern</u>, and <u>affordable</u>.

                         verb   +   verb

3. For over twenty years, guests have <u>stayed</u> here and <u>enjoyed</u> our comfortable rooms.

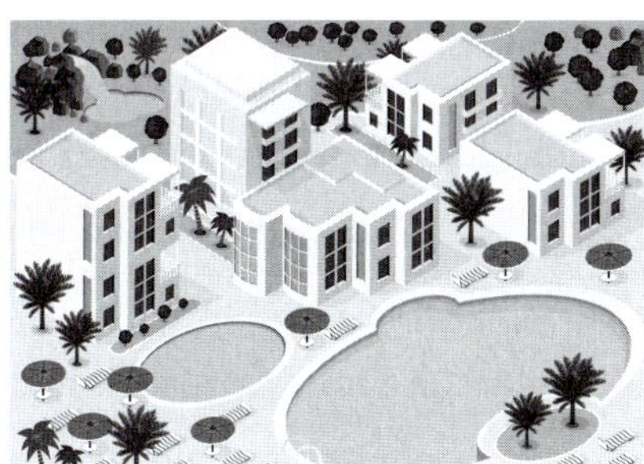

4. Our guests use our swimming pool, tennis courts, and gym.

5. All rooms have a microwave, refrigerator, and coffee maker.

6. There is no charge for parking and high-speed internet.

7. This year we remodeled our hotel and added a new restaurant.

8. Now our guests can enjoy fresh and delicious meals.

9. We also host weddings and other special events.

10. Our staff is friendly, helpful, and professional.

PRACTICE 2 ▶ Punctuating sentences. (Chart 8-1)

Each of these sentences contains two independent clauses. Find the subject "S" and verb "V" of each clause. Add a comma or a period. Capitalize as necessary.

       S   V   S   V

1. a. Birds fly, and fish swim.

       S   V   S   V

   b. Birds fly. fish swim.

2. a. Dogs bark lions roar.

   b. Dogs bark and lions roar.

3. a. A week has seven days a year has 365 days.

   b. A week has seven days and a year has 365 days.

4. a. Ahmed raised his hand and the teacher pointed at him.

   b. Ahmed raised his hand the teacher pointed at him.

PRACTICE 3 ▶ Punctuating items connected with *and.* (Chart 8-1)

Add commas where necessary. Write *No change* if no change is necessary.

1. a. I opened the door and walked into the room. *No change.*

   b. I opened the door**,** walked into the room**,** and sat down at my desk.

2. a. Their flag is green and black.

   b. Their flag is green black and yellow.

3. a. Tom ate a sandwich and drank a glass of juice.

   b. Tom made a sandwich poured a glass of juice and sat down to eat his lunch.

4. a. Ms. Parker is intelligent friendly and kind.

   b. Mr. Parker is grouchy and unhappy.

5. a. I sent text messages to Lily Daniel Joe and Emma.

   b. I always read the newspaper online and listen to a podcast in the morning.

   c. Can you watch TV listen to a podcast and check text messages at the same time?

PRACTICE 4 ▶ Punctuating sentences. (Chart 8-1)

Write "C" if the punctuation is correct and "I" for incorrect. Make the necessary corrections.

1. a. _____ Amy jogged along the road I rode my bicycle.

   b. _____ Amy stopped after 20 minutes. I continued on for an hour.

2. a. _____ Trained dogs can lie down and perform other tricks on command.

   b. _____ My mom trained our dog to sit, my dad trained it to bark at strangers.

3. a. _____ The river rose, it flooded the towns in the valley.

   b. _____ The river and streams rose. They flooded the towns and farms in the valley.

4. a. _____ Astrology is the study of the stars, planets and their effect on our lives.

   b. _____ Sharon reads her horoscope every day. She believes the positions of the stars and planets affect her daily life.

   c. _____ Sharon's children don't believe in astrology, they don't listen to the information she gives them.

PRACTICE 5 ▶ Connecting ideas with *and.* (Chart 8-1)

Part I. Read the passage.

Very Old Twins

Kin Narita and Gin Kanie were twin sisters from Japan. They were born in 1892. Their family name was Yano. Their first names are names of valuable metals: silver and gold. Kin means silver and Gin means gold.

They were 99 years old when the mayor of Nagoya, their hometown, visited them. He visited them on a national holiday—Respect for the Aged Day. In Japan, many people live a long time and receive a lot of respect when they are old. The mayor congratulated the twins on their long and healthy lives.

After the mayor's visit, the twins became famous and popular. They appeared on television game shows and in advertisements. People liked their wide smiles and their lively interest in the world. They laughed and smiled a lot. They said they stayed healthy because they had a simple lifestyle, walked everywhere, and enjoyed people, especially each other.

Kin had 11 children, and Gin had five children. They had many grandchildren and great-grandchildren. Kin died in January, 2000, at the age of 107, and Gin died in February, 2001, at the age of 108.

Part II. Each statement is incorrect. Make true statements. Write the correct punctuation.

1. The twins' first names mean health and happiness.

   The twins' first names mean silver and gold.

2. In Japan, many people don't live a long time, and they don't receive respect when they are old.

   ____

3. The twins were young and sick.

   ____

4. The twins rarely laughed and smiled.

   ____

5. The twins never had a simple lifestyle and always drove everywhere.

   ____

6. They didn't enjoy people and they didn't enjoy each other.

   ____

7. Kin and Gin didn't have any children or grandchildren.

   ____

8. When they died Kin and Gin were together.

   ____

PRACTICE 6 ▸ Using *but* and *or*. (Chart 8-2)

Add commas where necessary. Write ***No change*** if no change is necessary.

1. I talked to Camila for a long time**,** but she didn't listen.
2. I talked to Martin for a long time and asked him many questions. *No change.*
3. Please email Jane or Ted.
4. Please email Jane and Ted.
5. Please email Jane Ted or Anna.
6. Please email Jane Ted and Anna.
7. Did you text Kim or Luis?
8. I didn't text Leo Sarah or Hugo.
9. I waved at my friend but she didn't see me.
10. I waved at my friend and she waved back.

PRACTICE 7 ▸ Using *and, but, or,* and *so.* (Charts 8-1 → 8-3)

Choose the correct answers.

1. I was tired, ______ I went to bed.

   a. but   b. or   c. so

2. I lay down on the couch ______ took a nap.

   a. but   b. and   c. so

3. The students were on time, ______ the teacher was late.

   a. but   b. or   c. so

4. I want a pet. I'd like to have a cat _____ a dog.

    a. but   b. and   c. or

5. Our kids are happy _____ healthy.

    a. but   b. and   c. or

6. I wanted a cup of tea, _____ I boiled some water.

    a. but   b. and   c. so

7. My phone rang, _____ I didn't answer it.

    a. but   b. and   c. so

8. You can have an apple _____ an orange. Choose one.

    a. but   b. and   c. or

PRACTICE 8 ▸ Connecting ideas with *so*. (Chart 8-3)

Complete each sentence with a correct phrase from the list.

a. everybody laughed	e. she doesn't walk yet
b. I didn't leave a message	f. she walks and runs everywhere
c. I left a message	g. the grass got brown and dry
d. nobody laughed	h. the grass was green and bright

1. The joke was very funny, so _____.

2. The joke wasn't funny, so _____.

3. It didn't rain all summer, so _____.

4. It rained a lot this summer, so _____.

5. Our baby is only three months old, so _____.

6. Our baby is two years old, so _____.

7. Jackson didn't answer his phone, so _____.

8. Paul never checks his voicemail, so _____.

PRACTICE 9 ▸ Using *and*, *but*, *or*, and *so*. (Charts 8-1 → 8-3)

Write "C" if the punctuation is correct and "I" for incorrect. Make the necessary corrections.

1. _____ I washed and dried the dishes.

2. _____ I washed the dishes, and my son dried them.

3. _____ Victor offered me an apple or a peach.

4. _____ I bought some apples peaches and bananas.

5. _____ I was hungry so I ate a sandwich.

6. _____ Carlos was hungry and ate two sandwiches.

7. _____ My sister is generous and kind-hearted.

8. _____ My daughter is shy caring independent and smart.

Add periods, commas, and capital letters as necessary. Don't change any of the words or the order of the words.

1. James has a cold. *H*he needs to rest and drink plenty of fluids**,** so he should go to bed and drink juice or water he needs to sleep a lot so he shouldn't drink fluids with caffeine, such as tea coffee or cola.

2. The normal pulse for an adult is between 60 and 80 beats per minute but exercise fear excitement and a fever will all make a pulse beat faster the normal pulse for a child is around 80 to 90.

3. Edward Fox was a park ranger for 35 years during that time, he was hit by lightning eight times the lightning never killed him but it burned his skin and damaged his hearing.

Add commas where necessary. Some sentences need no commas.

An English School for Gina

   Gina wants a job as an air traffic controller. Every air traffic controller worldwide uses English so it is important for her to become fluent in the language. She has decided to take some intensive English courses at a private language institute but she isn't sure which one to attend. There are many schools available and they offer many different kinds of classes. She has also heard of air traffic control schools that include English as part of their coursework but she needs to have a fairly high level of English to attend. She has to decide soon or the classes will be full. She's planning to visit her top three choices this summer and decide on the best one for her.

Complete the sentences with the correct auxiliary verbs.

1. Alex didn't study for the test, but Hannah _______*did*_______.

2. Alice doesn't come to class every day, but Julie _____________.

3. Zac went to the movie last night, but I _____________.

4. I don't live in the dorm, but Rob and Jim _____________.

5. My roommate was at home last night, but I _____________.

6. Mr. Wong isn't here today, but Miss Choki _____________.

7. Susan won't be at the meeting tonight, but I _____________.

8. Susan isn't going to go to the meeting tonight, but I _____________.

9. I'll be there, but she _____________.

10. I haven't finished my work yet, but Erica _____________.

11. My sister enjoys action movies, but I _____________.

12. I enjoy romantic comedies, but my sister _____________.

Complete the sentences with the correct auxiliary verbs.

1. Rob lives in the dorm, and Jim _________________ too.

2. I don't live in the dorm, and Caroline _________________ either.

3. Ted isn't here today, and Lindsey _________________ either.

4. The teacher is listening to the recording, and the students _________________ too.

5. I'll be there, and Mike _________________ too.

6. I can speak French, and my wife _________________ too.

7. Jane would like a cup of coffee, and I _________________ too.

8. I like rock music, and my roommate _________________ too.

9. Paul can't speak Spanish, and Chris _________________ either.

10. I am exhausted from the long trip, and my mother _________________ too.

11. I have a dimple in my chin, and my brother _________________ too.

12. I visited the museum yesterday, and my friend _________________ too.

PRACTICE 14 ▶ Using *and + too, so, either, neither.* (Chart 8-5)
Complete the sentences by using the word in *italics* and an appropriate auxiliary.

1. *Tom*   Jack has a mustache, and so ______*does Tom*______.

   Jack has a mustache, and ______*Tom does*______ too.

2. *Brian*   David doesn't have a mustache, and neither _________________.

   David doesn't have a mustache, and _________________ either.

3. *I*   Maya was at home last night, and so _________________.

   Maya was at home last night, and _________________ too.

4. *Ray*   I went to a movie last night, and so _________________.

   I went to a movie last night, and _________________ too.

5. *Jason*   I didn't study last night, and neither _________________.

   I didn't study last night, and _________________ either.

6. *Rick*   Jim can't speak Arabic, and neither _________________.

   Jim can't speak Arabic, and _________________ either.

7. *Laura*   I like to go to science-fiction movies, and so _________________.

   I like to go to science-fiction movies, and _________________ too.

8. *Ava*   I don't like horror movies, and neither _________________.

   I don't like horror movies, and _________________ either.

PRACTICE 15 ▶ Using *and + too, so, either, neither.* (Chart 8-5)
Part I. Complete the sentences with an auxiliary + **too** or **either**.

1. I can't sew, and my roommate ________*can't either*________.

2. I don't like salty food, and my wife _________________.

3. Yesterday, Rosa came to class late and Nathan _________________.

4. Andy knew the answer to the question, and Tina _______________________.

5. I couldn't understand the substitute teacher, and Yoko _______________________.

6. I'd rather stay home this evening, and my husband _______________________.

Part II. Complete the sentences with an auxiliary + ***so*** or ***neither***.

7. Pasta is a famous Italian dish, and ______*so is*______ pizza.

8. I didn't go to the bank, and _______________________ my husband.

9. I'm not a native speaker of English, and _______________________ Mr. Chu.

10. I've never seen a monkey in the wild, and _______________________ my children.

11. When we heard the hurricane warning, I nailed boards over my windows, and

    _______________________ all of my neighbors.

12. My brother and I are taking the same chemistry course. It is difficult, but I like it and

    _______________________ he.

PRACTICE 16 ▸ Auxiliary verbs after *but* and *and*. (Charts 8-4 and 8-5)

A woman is talking about her housemate, Hanna. Choose the correct answers.

1. I like cooking, and __*h*__.

2. I don't like housework, and Hanna _____.

3. I like gardening, and she _____.

4. I don't like snakes in our garden, and _____.

5. She likes to go jogging after work, and _____.

6. She doesn't like to play golf, and I _____.

7. She likes to watch old movies, and I _____.

8. She doesn't like to sleep late on weekends,
   and _____.

a. do too

b. does too

c. doesn't either

d. don't either

e. neither do I

f. neither does she

g. so do I

h. so does Hanna

PRACTICE 17 ▸ Connecting ideas with *because*. (Chart 8-6)

Add periods, commas, and capital letters as necessary.

1. Because his coffee was cold, Michael didn't finish it. *H* he left it on the table and walked away.

2. I opened the window because the room was hot a nice breeze came in.

3. Because the weather was bad we canceled our trip into the city we stayed home and watched TV.

4. Gabi loves gymnastics because she hopes to be on an Olympic team she practices hard every day.

5. Francisco is very good in math because several colleges want him to attend they are offering him full

   scholarships.

PRACTICE 18 ▶ Connecting ideas with *because*. (Chart 8-6)

Read each pair of phrases and circle the one that gives the reason (explains "why"). Then check the correct sentence.

1. (lose weight,) go on a diet

   ✔ Eric went on a diet because he wanted to lose weight.

   _____ Because Eric went on a diet, he wanted to lose weight.

2. didn't have money, couldn't buy food

   _____ The family couldn't buy food because they didn't have money.

   _____ Because the family couldn't buy food, they didn't have money.

3. work long hours, aren't home very much

   _____ Because our neighbors work long hours, they aren't home very much.

   _____ Our neighbors work long hours because they aren't home very much.

4. go to bed, be tired

   _____ I am tired because I am going to bed.

   _____ Because I am tired, I am going to bed.

5. be in great shape, exercise every day

   _____ Because Sofia exercises every day, she is in great shape.

   _____ Sofia exercises every day because she is in great shape.

6. have a high fever, go to the doctor

   _____ Because Jennifer has a high fever, she is going to the doctor.

   _____ Jennifer has a high fever because she is going to the doctor.

PRACTICE 19 ▶ Using *so* or *because*. (Charts 8-3 and 8-6)

Complete the sentences with **so** or **because**. Add commas where appropriate. Capitalize as necessary.

1. a. He was hungry ___, so___ he ate a sandwich.

   b. ___Because___ he was hungry, he ate a sandwich.

   c. He ate a sandwich _____ he was hungry.

2. a. _____ my sister was tired she went to bed.

   b. My sister went to bed _____ she was tired.

   c. My sister was tired _____ she went to bed.

3. a. Sam worked hard _____ he got a promotion.

   b. _____ he worked hard Sam got a promotion.

   c. Sam got a promotion _____ he worked hard.

4. a. Olivia has a meeting _____ she'll be home late tonight.

   b. Olivia will be home late tonight _____ she has a meeting.

   c. _____ she has a meeting, Olivia will be home late tonight.

5. a. Students can usually identify Italy easily on a world map ________________ it is
shaped like a boot.

   b. ________________ Italy has the shape of a boot students can usually identify it easily.

   c. Italy has the shape of a boot ________________ students can usually identify it easily on a map.

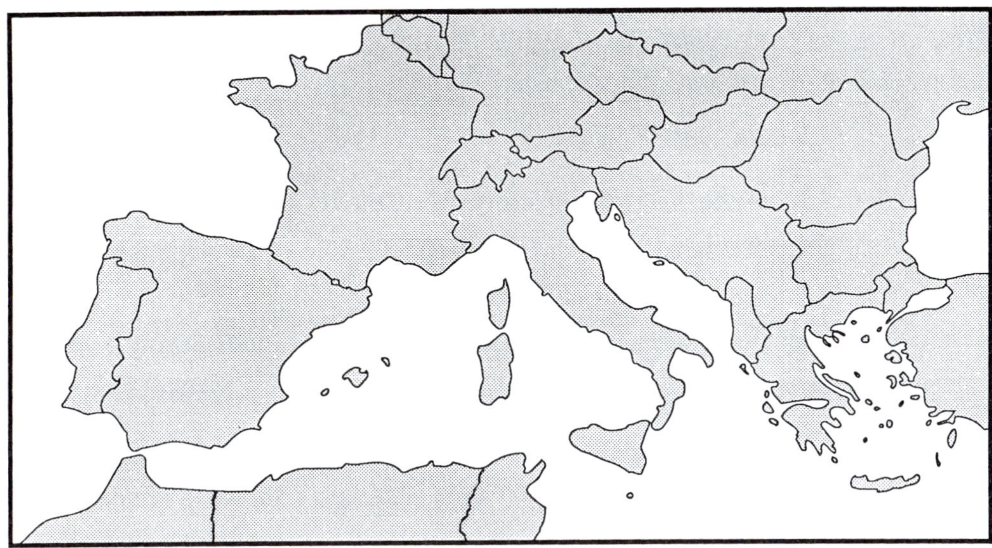

PRACTICE 20 ▸ Connecting ideas with *even though / although.* (Chart 8-7)

Complete each sentence with the correct form of the verb in *italics.* Some verbs will be negative.

1. Even though I (*like*) ______*like*______ fish, I don't eat it much.

2. Even though I (*like*) ______*don't like*______ vegetables, I eat them every day.

3. Although my hairdresser (*be*) ________________ expensive, I go to her once a month.

4. Even though the basketball game was over, the fans (*stay*) ________________ in their
   seats cheering.

5. Although my clothes were wet from the rain, I (*change*) ________________ them.

6. Even though Kai studied for weeks, he (*pass*) ________________ his exams.

7. Even though the soup was salty, everyone (*eat*) ________________ it.

8. Although the roads (*be*) ________________ icy, no one got in an accident.

PRACTICE 21 ▸ Using *because* and *even though.* (Charts 8-6 and 8-7)

Choose the correct answers.

1. Even though I was hungry, I ______ a lot at dinner.

   a. ate   b. didn't eat

2. Because I was hungry, I ______ a lot at dinner.

   a. ate   b. didn't eat

3. Because I was cold, I ______ my coat.

   a. put on   b. didn't put on

4. Even though I was cold, I ______ my coat.

   a. put on   b. didn't put on

5. Even though Mike _______ sleepy, he stayed up to watch the end of the game on TV.

   a. was   b. wasn't

6. Because Lesley _______ sleepy, she went to bed.

   a. was   b. wasn't

7. Because Kate ran too slowly, she _______ the race.

   a. won   b. didn't win

8. Even though Jessica ran fast, she _______ the race.

   a. won   b. didn't win

PRACTICE 22 ▸ Using *because* and *even though*. (Charts 8-6 and 8-7)

Complete the sentences with **because** or **even though**.

1. Yuko went to a dentist ______*because*______ she had a toothache.

2. Colette didn't go to a dentist ____________________ she had a toothache.

3. Julia went to a dentist ____________________ she didn't have a toothache. She just wanted a checkup.

4. Louie didn't wash his shirt ____________________ it was dirty.

5. Eric washed his shirt ____________________ it was dirty.

6. ____________________ Claire lives in Mexico, she doesn't speak Spanish.

7. ____________________ Mateo lived in Saudi Arabia for ten years, he speaks Arabic.

8. ____________________ Mateo speaks Arabic, he can't read or write it very well.

9. ____________________ Nick studied for hours, he didn't pass the exam.

10. ____________________ Jasmine prepared for her exam, she got a very high score.

PRACTICE 23 ▸ Using *because* and *although*. (Charts 8-6 and 8-7)

Complete the paragraphs with **because** or **although**.

It's difficult to open some pill bottles ____________________
                                                  1
they have child-proof caps. Pill manufacturers make this type of bottle

____________________ they don't want children to open the bottles
        2
and eat the pills. The pills inside the bottle are often attractive, and

____________________ they look like candy, they are not candy.
        3

Last week there was a story in the news about a lucky baby. The baby

found an open bottle of medicine. ____________________ the pills looked just like candy, he
                                            4
started to eat them. When his mother walked into the room, she saw her baby and the open bottle.

____________________ she was frightened, she acted calmly. She immediately took the baby to the
        5
emergency room at the nearby hospital. ____________________ the baby had eaten pills for adults,
                                                   6
he needed only minor treatment. The mother saved her baby ____________________ she
                                                                        7
had acted quickly.

Choose the best answers.

1. I gave him the money because ___c___.

    a. I didn't want to

    b. he had a lot of money

    c. I owed it to him

2. Although ______, the hungry man ate every bit of it.

    a. the bread was old and stale

    b. the cheese tasted good to him

    c. an apple is both nutritious and delicious

3. The nurse didn't bring Mr. Hill a glass of water even though ______.

    a. she was very busy

    b. she forgot

    c. he asked her three times

4. When she heard the loud crash, Marge ran outside in the snow although ______.

    a. her mother ran out with her

    b. she wasn't wearing any shoes

    c. she ran as fast as she could

5. Even though his shoes were wet and muddy, Brian ______.

    a. took them off at the front door

    b. walked right into the house and across the carpet

    c. wore wool socks

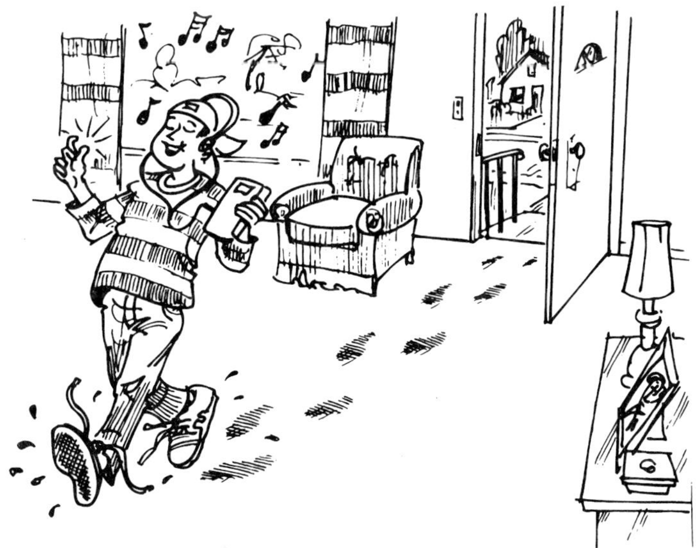

6. Alex got on the bus in front of his hotel. He was on his way to the art museum. Because he _____,
   he asked the bus driver to tell him where to get off.

   a. was late for work and didn't want his boss to get mad

   b. was carrying a heavy suitcase

   c. was a tourist and didn't know the city streets very well

7. Although _____, Eric got on the plane.

   a. he is married

   b. he is afraid of flying

   c. the flight attendant welcomed him aboard

8. When I attended my first business conference out of town, I felt very uncomfortable during the
   social events because _____.

   a. we were all having a good time

   b. I didn't know anyone there

   c. I know a lot about business

9. Everyone listened carefully to what the speaker was saying even though _____.

   a. they had printed copies of the speech in their hands

   b. she spoke loudly and clearly

   c. the speech was very interesting

10. Talil works in the city, but once a month he visits his mother, who lives in the country. He has to
    rent a car for these trips because _____.

    a. it is expensive

    b. he doesn't have a driver's license

    c. he doesn't own a car

PRACTICE 25 ▸ Check your knowledge. (Chapter 8 Review)

Correct the errors.

1. I don't drink coffee, and my roommate ~~isn't~~ *doesn't* either.

2. The flight was overbooked, I had to fly on another airline.

3. Many people use their phones to post pictures on social media check email and watch videos.

4. Even my father works two jobs, he always has time to play soccer or baseball on the weekends with his family.

5. I saw a bad accident and my sister too.

6. Oscar always pays his bills on time but his brother wasn't.

7. Because my mother is afraid of heights, I took her up to the observation deck at the top of the building.

8. Janey doesn't like to get up early and either Joe.

9. My mother and my father. They immigrated to this country 30 years ago.

10. Even though Maya is very intelligent, her parents want to put her in an advanced program at school.

Circle the connecting words from Chapter 8 in the puzzle. The words may be horizontal, vertical, or diagonal. The first letter of each word is highlighted in green.

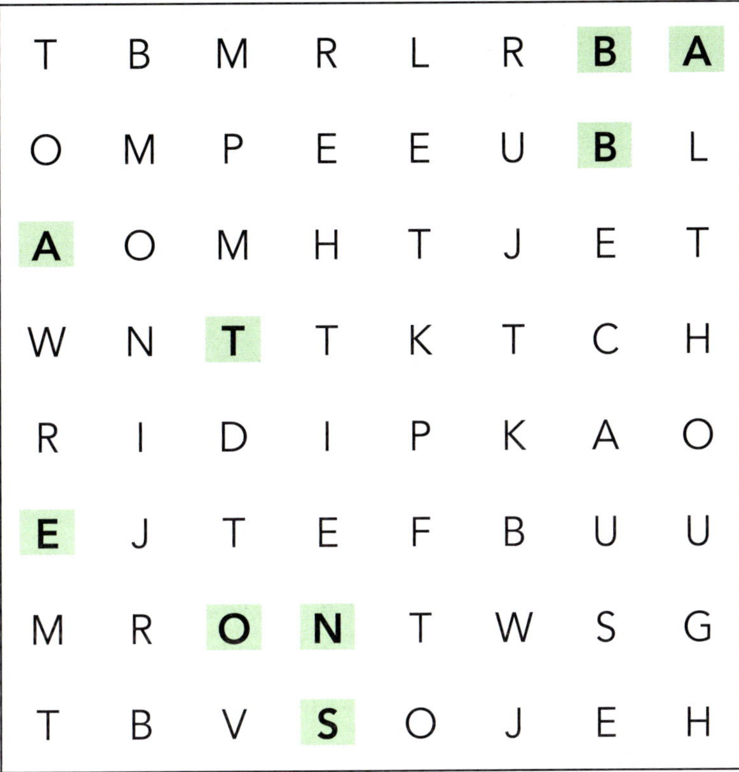

CHAPTER 9

Comparisons

PRACTICE 1 ▶ Comparative forms. (Chart 9-1)

Complete each sentence with the comparative form of the adjective.

1. The sun is (*large*) _______________ than the moon.

2. The moon is (*close*) _______________ to the earth than the sun.

3. Texas is (*hot*) _______________ than Colorado.

4. Alaska is (*cold*) _______________ than Hawaii.

5. A car is (*heavy*) _______________ than a bicycle.

6. Dolphins are (*intelligent*) _______________ than fish.

7. Traffic is (*bad*) _______________ in the morning than in the afternoon.

8. Public transportation (*good*) _______________ in large cities than in small towns.

PRACTICE 2 ▶ Comparative forms. (Chart 9-1)

Complete each sentence with the comparative form of the adjective.

1. Calculus is (*difficult*) _more difficult than_ algebra.

2. An airplane is (*expensive*) _more expensive than_ a car.

3. Which is (*large*) _larger_ : Greenland or Iceland?

4. Red or cayenne pepper tastes (*hot*) _hotter than_ black pepper.

5. Traffic is (*slow*) _more slowly than_ usual today. _slower than_

6. White chocolate is (*creamy*) _more creamy than_ dark chocolate because it has more fat. _creamier than_

7. Is smoking (*bad*) _worse than_ alcohol for your health?

8. A jaguar is (*fast*) _faster than_ a lion.

9. Which is (*important*) _more important than_ : happiness or wealth?

10. For long-distance trips, flying is (*quick*) _quicker than_ driving.

11. Which is (*heavy*) _heavier_ : a kilo of cotton or a kilo of rocks?*

12. My mother is a few years (*old*) _older than_ my father.

13. The month of February is (*short*) _shorter than_ March.

14. I can't carry your suitcase. It's (*heavy*) _heavier than_ mine.

15. A car is a lot (*expensive*) _more expensive than_ a bicycle.

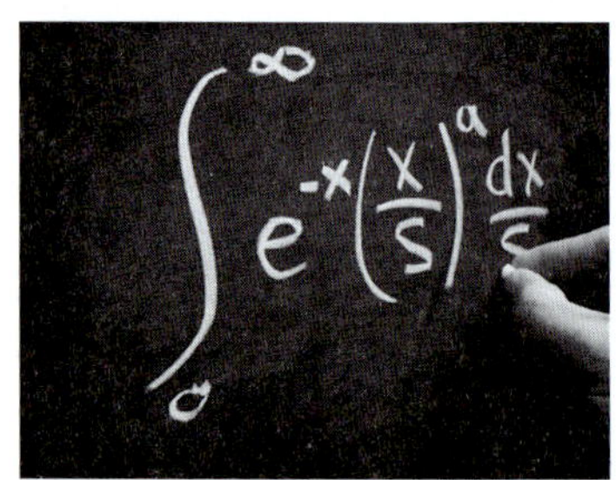

---

*This is a trick question.
Answer: They weigh the same.

Complete the sentences with the correct comparative form of the words from the box.

cheap	dry	foggy	high	sunny
cold	expensive	healthy	international	

1. Locations near the equator are hot. Locations near the North Pole and the South Pole are cold.

   For example, Siberia is much _______*colder*_______ than Cuba. The average temperature in Cuba is

   a lot _______*higher*_______ than the average temperature in Siberia.

2. Some places in northern Europe are often foggy. London is famous for its fog. It's much

   _______________ in London than it is in southern Europe. The island of Majorca, in southern

   Spain, is very sunny. It's a lot _______________ in Majorca than it is in London.

3. Some people with illnesses have to move to places with dry air. For example, my uncle moved from

   Chicago to Arizona because the air in Arizona is a lot _______________ than it is in Chicago.

   The air in Arizona was good for him, and he became a lot _______________ there.

4. New York is an international city. My hometown is just a small town. New York is much

   _______________ than my hometown. It's expensive to live in New York. It's far

   _______________ to live in New York than it is to live in my hometown. It's much

   _______________ to live in my hometown than it is to live in New York.

PRACTICE 4 ▸ Superlative forms. (Chart 9-2)

Complete the sentences with the given ideas and the superlative form.

bad flood	common word	intelligent animals
big organ	good policy	large continent
close planet	high level	tall mountain

1. Mount McKinley in Alaska is _______*the tallest mountain*_______ in North America.

2. The skin is _______________ in the human body. It covers the largest area.

3. *The* is _______________ in the English language.

4. Mercury is _______________ to the sun.

5. Asia is _______________ on earth.

6. Bottle-nosed dolphins are _______________ in the sea.

7. Last spring, the towns on the river experienced _______________ of this century. The

   water rose to _______________ in the towns' history.

8. A famous proverb, and a rule for living, is "Honesty is _______________." It means

   that you should always be honest.

PRACTICE 5 ▸ Comparatives and superlatives. (Charts 9-1 and 9-2)

Complete the sentences with **better**, **the best**, **worse**, or **the worst**.

1. I just finished a terrible book. It's _______*the worst*_______ book I've ever read.

2. The weather was bad yesterday, but it's terrible today. The weather is _______*worse*_______ today

   than it was yesterday.

3. This cake is really good. It's _________________ cake I've ever eaten.

4. My grades this term are great. They're much _________________ than last term.

5. Being separated from my family in time of war is one of _________________ experiences
   I can imagine.

6. I broke my nose in a football game yesterday. Today it's very painful. For some reason, the pain is
   _________________ today than it was yesterday.

7. The fire spread and burned down an entire city block. It was _________________ fire we've ever
   had in our town.

8. I think my cold is almost over. I feel a lot _________________ than I did yesterday. I can finally
   breathe again.

PRACTICE 6 ▸ Comparative and superlative forms. (Charts 9-2 and 9-3)

Write the comparative and superlative forms of the given words.

Comparative	Superlative
1. strong *stronger*	*the strongest*
2. important *more important*	*the most important*
3. soft	
4. lazy	
5. wonderful	
6. calm	
7. low	
8. thin	
9. convenient	
10. simple	
11. good	
12. bad	
13. famous	
14. slow	
15. slowly	

PRACTICE 7 ▸ Completing comparisons with pronouns. (Chart 9-3)

Complete the sentences with a pronoun and the correct auxiliary verb. Use both formal and
informal completions.

1. Jacob woke up at nine. I woke up at six.

   He slept later than _______ *I did* _______ / _______ *me* _______.

2. Henry is a good soccer player. Layla is better.

   She is a better soccer player than _______ *he is* _______ / _______ *him* _______.

3. I won the race. Anna came in second.

   I ran faster than _________________ / _________________.

4. My parents were nervous about my motorcycle ride. I was just a little nervous.

   They were a lot more nervous than _________________ / _________________.

5. My aunt will stay with us for two weeks. My uncle has to return home to his job after

   a couple of days.

   She will be here with us a lot longer than _________________ / _________________.

6. I've been here for two years. Sam has been here for two months.

   I've been here a lot longer than _________________ / _________________.

7. I have a brother. His name is David. He's really tall. I'm just medium height.

   He's taller than _________________ / _________________.

8. My brother is sixteen. I'm seventeen.

   I'm older than _________________ / _________________.

9. My sister is really athletic. I don't really like sports.

   She's a lot more athletic than _________________ / _________________.

10. I'm a very good student, though. My sister isn't interested in school.

   I'm more studious than _________________ / _________________.

PRACTICE 8 ▸ Completing superlatives. (Chart 9-3)

Part I. Complete the sentences with superlatives and the appropriate word: *in, of,* or *ever.*

1. Economics is (*difficult*) ___the most difficult___ course I have ______ever______ taken.

2. For me, English is (*easy*) _________________ course I have _________________ taken.

3. A lot of students take a course called *The History of Rap Music* because it is one of (*interesting*)

   _________________ courses _________________ the college.

4. The professor who teaches it is excellent. He is one of (*good*) _________________ professors

   _________________ all the professors in the college.

5. My friends say that my grandmother is (*wise*) _________________ person they have

   _________________ met.

6. My wife won our town's annual marathon race twice. She was (*fast*) _________________

   runner _________________ all.

7. My cousin Carolina has won a scholarship to Harvard University to study mathematics. She is one

   of (*brilliant*) _________________ mathematics students _________________ the whole

   country.

8. One of (*successful*) _________________ business people _________________ our town is

   Mitchell Brown, the owner of our only independent bookstore.

9. He established the store ten years ago, and now it is (*busy*) _________________ bookstore

   _________________ our area.

10. Mitchell is not only a successful businessperson, but he is one of (*generous*)

_______________________ people that our town has _______________________

known. He has given a lot of time and money to local charities.

11. Mitchell believes that contributing to the quality of life in his

community is (*important*) _______________________ thing that he can

do _______________________ life.

12. My three kids all have artistic talent, but Liam is (*artistic*)

_______________________ all.

PRACTICE 9 ▸ Comparative adjectives and adverbs. (Charts 9-1 and 9-4)

Write the correct comparative form of the adjective or adverb in each sentence. If the word is an adjective, circle ADJ. If it is an adverb, circle ADV.

1. *slow*
   slowly

   I like to drive fast, but my brother William doesn't. As a rule, he drives

   _______*more slowly*_______ than I do.   ADJ   (ADV)

2. *slow*
   slowly

   Alex is a _______*slower*_______ driver than I am.   (ADJ)   ADV

3. *serious*
   seriously

   Some workers are _______________________ about their jobs than others.   ADJ   ADV

4. *serious*
   seriously

   Some workers approach their jobs _______________________ than others.   ADJ   ADV

5. *polite*
   politely

   Why do my kids behave _______________________ at other people's houses

   than at home?   ADJ   ADV

6. *polite*
   politely

   Why are they _______________________ at their friends' houses than at home?   ADJ   ADV

7. *careful*
   carefully

   I'm a cautious person when I express my opinions, but my sister will say anything

   to anyone. I'm much _______________________ when I speak to others than my

   sister is.   ADJ   ADV

8. *careful*
   carefully

   I always speak _______________________ in public than my sister does.   ADJ   ADV

9. *clear*
   clearly

   I can't understand Mark's father very well when he talks, but I can understand Mark.

   He speaks much _______________________ than his father.   ADJ   ADV

10. *clear*
    clearly

    Mark is a much _______________________ speaker than his father.   ADJ   ADV

PRACTICE 10 ▸ *Farther* and *further*. (Chart 9-4)

Choose the correct answers. More than one answer may be correct.

1. The planet Earth is ___________ from the sun than the planet Mercury is.

   a. farther   b. further

2. I have no ___________ need of this equipment. I'm going to sell it.

   a. farther   b. further

3. I'm tired. I walked ___________ than I wanted to.

   a. farther   b. further

4. I'll be available by phone if you have any ___________ questions.

   a. farther   b. further

5. A: Tell us more.

   B: Sorry, I have no ___________ comment.

   a. farther   b. further

6. A: I heard that you and Tom are engaged to be married.

   B: Nothing could be ___________ from the truth!

   a. farther   b. further

PRACTICE 11 ▸ Repeating a comparative. (Chart 9-5)

Complete the sentences with words from the box. Repeat the comparative.

| bad | big | expensive | friendly | ✓good | long | mad | noisy | warm |

1. Joseph's health is improving. He's getting ___*better and better*___.

2. The Davidsons just had their sixth child. Their family is getting _______________.

3. People are worried about the environment. The ice at the North and South poles is melting because

   the earth is getting _______________.

4. This neighborhood used to be quiet, but since some new restaurants opened nearby, it is getting

   _______________.

5. I was really angry! I got _______________ until my brother touched my arm and told

   me to calm down.

6. We were so glad we had arrived early at the ticket office. As we waited for it to open, the line got

   _______________.

7. Textbooks are costly. They are getting _______________ every year.

8. When Maya first came into our class, she was very shy. She didn't talk to anyone. But little by little,

   she has relaxed, and now she is getting _______________.

9. The weather is getting _______________. The airport has canceled most flights

   because of the snowstorm.

PRACTICE 12 ▸ Double comparatives. (Chart 9-5)
Complete the sentences with double comparatives.

1. I exercise every day. Exercise makes me strong. The ___*more*___ I exercise, the ___*stronger*___ I get.
2. If butter is soft, it is easy to spread on bread. The ______________ the butter is, the ______________ it is to spread on bread.
3. I'm trying to make my life simpler. It makes me feel more relaxed. The ______________ I make my life, the ______________ I feel.
4. I spend a long time each day looking at a computer screen. My eyes get very tired. The ______________ I look at a computer screen, the ______________ my eyes get.
5. When the wind blows hard, it whistles through the trees. The ______________ the wind blows, the ______________ it whistles through the trees.

PRACTICE 13 ▸ Double comparatives. (Chart 9-5)
Complete the sentences with double comparatives, using the ideas in parentheses.

1. (*She talked. She got excited.*)

   I met a woman at a party last night. She told us many stories about her exciting job as a wildlife photographer. The ______________, ______________.

2. (*He talked. I got hungry.*)

   I also met a man who is a chef. He talked about some of the great meals he makes. I got hungry just listening to him. The ______________, ______________.

3. (*You are old. You understand more.*)

   There are many advantages to being young, but the ______________, ______________.

4. (*Bill talked very fast. I became confused.*)

   Bill was trying to explain some complicated physics problems to help me prepare for an exam. He kept talking faster and faster. The ______________, ______________.

5. (*The fans clapped and cheered. The basketball team made more shots.*)

   The fans in the arena were excited and noisy, and it seemed to make their team play better. The ______________, ______________.

PRACTICE 14 ▸ Modifying comparatives with adjectives and adverbs. (Chart 9-6)
Choose the correct answers. More than one answer may be correct.

1. This phone is not __________ expensive.

   a. very   b. a lot   c. much   d. far

2. That phone is __________ more expensive than this one.

   a. very   b. a lot   c. much   d. far

3. My nephew is __________ polite.

   a. very   b. a lot   c. much   d. far

4. My nephew is __________ more polite than my niece.

   a. very   b. a lot   c. much   d. far

5. Ted is __________ taller than his brother.

   a. very   b. a lot   c. much   d. far

6. Ted is __________ tall.

   a. very   b. a lot   c. much   d. far

7. I think astronomy is __________ more interesting than geology.

   a. very   b. a lot   c. much   d. far

8. I think astronomy is __________ interesting.

   a. very   b. a lot   c. much   d. far

9. It took me a lot longer to get over my cold than it took you to get over your cold.

   My cold was __________ worse than yours.

   a. very   b. a lot   c. much   d. far

PRACTICE 15 ▶ Negative comparatives. (Chart 9-7)

Choose the sentence that is closest in meaning to the given sentence.

1. I've never taken a harder test in this class.

   (a.) The test was hard.

   b. The test wasn't hard.

2. I've never taken a hard test in this class.

   a. The tests in this class are hard.

   b. The tests in this class aren't hard.

3. Professor Jones has never given a difficult test.

   a. His tests are difficult.

   b. His tests aren't difficult.

4. Professor Smith has never given a more difficult test.

   a. The test was difficult.

   b. The test wasn't difficult.

5. There have never been worse economic conditions in Leadville.

   a. Leadville has bad economic conditions.

   b. Leadville doesn't have bad economic conditions.

6. There have never been bad economic conditions in Leadville.

   a. Leadville has bad economic conditions.

   b. Leadville doesn't have bad economic conditions.

7. We've never stayed in a more comfortable hotel room.

   a. The room was comfortable.

   b. The room wasn't comfortable.

8. We've never stayed in a comfortable room at that hotel.

   a. The rooms are comfortable.

   b. The rooms aren't comfortable.

Complete the sentences with the comparative and superlative forms of the words in *italics*.

1. Pierre told a really *funny* story. It is ______*the funniest*______ story I've ever heard (in my life).
   I've never heard a ______*funnier*______ story (than that one).

2. John felt very *sad* when he saw the child begging for money. In fact, he has never felt
   ________________________ (than he did then). That is ________________________ he has ever felt
   (in his life).

3. Jan just finished a really *good* book. She thinks it was ________________________ book she has ever
   read. She says that she has never read a ________________________ book.

4. The villagers fought the rising flood all through the night. They were *exhausted* the next morning.
   They have never had a ________________________ experience. That was ________________________
   experience they have ever had.

5. When her daughter was born, Rachel felt extremely *happy*. In fact, she has never felt
   ________________________ (than she did then). That was ________________________ she has ever felt
   (in her life).

6. Oscar told a very *entertaining* story after dinner. In fact, he has never told a ________________________
   story. It is one of ________________________ stories I have ever heard in my life.

7. Mari studied very *hard* for her college entrance exams. In fact, she has never studied
   ________________________. That was ________________________ she has ever studied in her life.

8. The weather is really *hot* today! In fact, so far this year the weather has never been
   ________________________. This is ________________________ weather we've had so far this year.

Make comparisons using **as ... as**.

1. Sidney is very busy. Jason is very busy.
   → Sidney is ______*(just) as busy as Jason (is)*______.

2. Sidney is not very busy at all. Jason is very, very busy.
   → Sidney is not ______*(nearly) as busy as Jason (is)*______.

3. I was tired. Susan was very tired.
   → I wasn't ____*nearly as tired as Susan.*____.

4. Adam wasn't tired at all. Susan was very tired.
   → Adam wasn't ____*nearly as tired as Susan*____.

5. Ashley is lazy. Her sister Amanda is equally lazy.
   → Ashley is ________________________.

6. Their brother Alan is extremely lazy.
   → Ashley and Amanda are lazy, but they are not ________________________.

Make comparisons using **as ... as** and the adjective in parentheses. Use **not** as necessary.

1. Adults have more strength than children. (*strong*)

   → Children ______*aren't as strong as*______ adults.

2. Tom and Jerry are the same height. (*tall*)

   → Tom ___________________________ Jerry.

3. Dr. Green has a little money. Dr. Brown has a lot of money. (*wealthy*)

   → Dr. Green ___________________________ Dr. Brown.

4. City air is often polluted. Country air is often fresh and clear. (*polluted*)

   → Country air ___________________________ city air.

5. Paula studies a little bit. Jack studies a lot. (*studious*)

   → Paula ___________________________ Jack.

6. Math courses are easy for me, but language courses aren't. (*difficult*)

   → Math courses ___________________________ language courses for me.

PRACTICE 19 ▸ As ... as. (Chart 9-8)

Part I. Complete the sentences with one of the following:

- just as ... as
- almost as ... as / not quite as ... as
- not nearly as ... as

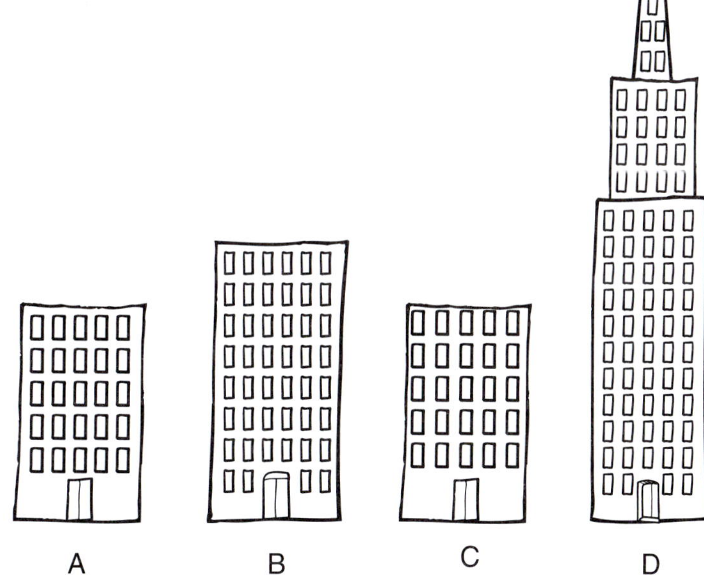

1. Building B is ______*not nearly as*______ high as Building D.

2. Building A is ___________________________ high as Building B.

3. Building C is ___________________________ high as Building D.

4. Building A is ___________________________ high as Building C.

Part II. Compare the arrival times. Meeting time: 9:00 A.M.

	Arrival times
David	9:01 A.M.
Julia	9:14 A.M.
Laura	9:15 A.M.
Paul	9:15 A.M.
James	9:25 A.M.

5. Paul was _______*just as*_______ late as Laura.

6. David was _____________________ late as James.

7. Julia was _____________________ late as Laura and Paul.

8. Julia was _____________________ late as James.

Part III. Compare world temperatures.

Bangkok	92°F / 33°C
Cairo	85°F / 30°C
Madrid	90°F / 32°C
Moscow	68°F / 20°C
Tokyo	85°F / 30°C

9. Tokyo is _____________________ hot as Cairo.

10. Moscow is _____________________ hot as Bangkok.

11. Madrid is _____________________ hot as Bangkok.

Part IV. Compare world temperatures today and yesterday.

	Yesterday	Today
Bangkok	95°F / 35°C	92°F / 33°C
Cairo	95°F / 35°C	85°F / 30°C
Madrid	90°F / 32°C	90°F / 32°C
Moscow	70°F / 21°C	68°F / 20°C
Tokyo	81°F / 27°C	85°F / 30°C

12. Cairo was _____________________ hot as Bangkok yesterday.

13. It's _____________________ warm in Moscow today as yesterday.

14. Madrid is _________________________ hot today as yesterday.

15. It was _________________________ hot in Tokyo yesterday as in Bangkok.

16. It's _________________________ hot in Bangkok today as yesterday.

PRACTICE 20 ▸ *As ... as.* (Chart 9-8)

Part I. Complete the expressions with the correct phrases from the box.

as a bat	as a picture	✓as ice
as a bird	as a pillow	✓as snow
as a flash	as dust	as ABC
as a mouse		

1. very white: as white _____*as snow*_____.

2. very cold: as cold _____*as ice*_____.

3. very pretty: as pretty _____*as a ~~bird~~ picture*_____.

4. can't see anything: as blind _____*as a bat?*_____.

5. very dry: as dry _____*as dust*_____.

6. very soft: as soft _____*as a ~~picture~~ pillow*_____.

7. very quick: as quick _____*as a ~~bird~~ flash*_____.

8. very quiet: as quiet _____*as a mouse.*_____.

9. very free: as free _____*as a bird*_____.

10. very simple: as simple _____*as ABC.*_____.

Part II. Complete the sentences with the given adjectives and the phrases from Part I.

blind	dry	pretty	quiet	soft
✓cold	free	quick	simple	white

11. Brrrr! Come inside. Your hands are freezing. They are as _____*cold as ice*_____.

12. I'm just running down to the corner store. I'll be back in a few minutes. I'll be as

_________________________.

13. I can't see anything without my glasses on. I'm as _________________________.

14. What laundry detergent do you use? Your white shirts were covered with dirt, and now they're so

clean and bright. They're as _________________________.

15. Shhh! Don't wake up Janet. She's sleeping on the couch. Be as _________________________.

16. Your little girl looks darling in that pink dress and hat. She looks as _________________________.

17. Don't worry. You'll pass your exams. You've been studying for weeks. It'll be as

_________________________ for you.

18. Charles looks so relaxed since he quit his job. He has no responsibilities for now. He must feel as

_________________________.

19. I have back problems and need to sleep on a bed that has a very firm mattress. My husband can

sleep on anything, even something that is as _________________________.

20. It hasn't rained in weeks. The grass is brown, and the flowers are dead. The ground is as

_________________________.

The passage contains nine phrases with ***not as …*** (***as***). <u>Underline</u> these phrases, and if possible, change them to sentences with the same meaning using ***less …*** (***than***).

A Move to a New Town

(1) Lia has been unhappy ever since she and her family moved to Southland, a suburb of a big city. She was very happy with her life in the city, where she had lived since she was born. She liked her friends, her school, and her neighborhood there.

less friendly than

(2) In her new school, the students are <u>not as friendly as</u> her old schoolmates. The classes are not as interesting as the ones in her old school, and she is a little bored. The classes are not as difficult, and she feels that she isn't learning much.

(3) She doesn't like her new neighborhood. It is not as convenient as her old neighborhood. In the city, all the stores were near her home. In the suburbs, the stores are not as close to her home as they were in the city. In the city, she didn't have to travel far to shop or go to a movie. Lia also misses the cultural events of the city. The cultural life in Southland is not as exciting as it is in the city, where she often went to concerts, plays, and interesting lectures.

(4) Lia is not as comfortable with her life now as she used to be. But she is not as unhappy as she was at first. She is working on changing her attitude. She is hoping that, with time, she will find that life in Southland is not as bad as she thought.

Complete the sentences with the correct words from the box. Use ***more*** to make the comparison.

days	paper	students	time	water
money	space	sugar	vegetables	winter clothes

1. Several people were absent yesterday, but everyone is here today. There are
   _______________________ in class today than there were yesterday.
2. I wanted to buy a new phone, but now I'm not sure. It's very expensive. It costs
   _______________________ than I thought.
3. Vanessa has a very healthy diet. She eats _______________________ than anyone I know.
4. Rami likes to drink very sweet tea. He adds _______________________ to his tea than most other people do.
5. February is the shortest month of the year. All the other months have _______________________ than February.
6. Your office is huge! I think it has _______________________ than the other offices in this building.

7. The printer is almost empty. We need _________________.

8. Alex is very busy this afternoon. Ask Anna to help you instead. She has _________________ than Alex.

9. I'm really thirsty. Could I have some _________________, please?

10. It's getting cold. We need to buy _________________ soon.

PRACTICE 23 ▸ Using *more* with adjectives, adverbs, and nouns. (Charts 9-1, 9-4, and 9-10)
Part I. **Adjectives**
Complete the sentences with the correct comparative form (***morel-er***).

difficult   loud   pleasant

1. A warm, sunny day is _________________ than a cold windy day.

2. Karen doesn't need a microphone when she speaks to the audience. She's the only person I know whose voice is _________________ than mine.

3. My course in microbiology is much _________________ than my biology course was.

Part II. **Adverbs**
Use the adverb forms of these adjectives.

careful   clear   fast

4. Your new phone is excellent, Joe. I can hear you much _________________ on this phone than on your old one.

5. Aunt Anna has been driving _________________ since she had her accident on the highway. In fact, she drives very slowly now, and she is quite nervous.

6. You can cook food in a microwave oven much _________________ than you can cook it in a regular oven. It takes only seven minutes to bake a potato, for example.

Part III. **Nouns**
Use the plural form of these nouns if necessary.

car   friend   homework   money   problem   snow

7. University students study hard. They have a lot _________________ than high school students.

8. There is far _________________ in winter in Alaska than there is in Texas.

9. I'm lonely. I wish I had _________________ to spend time with.

10. Sam's car is ten years old. He has _________________ with it than he did when it was new.

11. Traffic in this city has become a big problem. There are many _________________ on the road now than there were five years ago.

12. The economy is improving in this area. Small businesses made _________________ this year than they did last year.

Choose the correct answers.

1. I feel _____ in a plane than I do in a car.

   a. safe   b. more safer   c. safer

2. Mountain climbing takes _____ than walking on a level path.

   a. the more strength   b. the most strength   c. more strength

3. The _____ distance between two points is a straight line.

   a. shorter   b. more shorter   c. shortest

4. My grandfather feels _____ speaking his native language than he does speaking English.

   a. more comfortable   b. the more comfortable   c. the most comfortable

5. My friend has studied many languages. He thinks Japanese is _____ of all the languages
   he has studied.

   a. the more difficult   b. the most difficult   c. very difficult

6. I think learning a second language is _____ than learning chemistry or mathematics.

   a. more difficult   b. very difficult   c. the most difficult

7. One of _____ natural disasters in the world was the tsunami that happened in Asia in 2004.

   a. the worse   b. the worst   c. the most worse

8. In the United States, Florida produces _____ oranges of any state.

   a. more   b. the more   c. the most

9. It produces even _____ oranges than California does.

   a. more   b. the more   c. the most

10. Of all the countries in the world, Brazil produces _____ crop of oranges.

    a. the bigger   b. the more bigger   c. the biggest

PRACTICE 25 ▸ Review of comparatives and superlatives. (Charts 9-1 → 9-10)
Complete the sentences. Use any appropriate form of the words in parentheses and add any other
necessary words.

1. Sometimes I feel like all my friends are (*intelligent*) __more intelligent than__ I am, and yet,

   sometimes they tell me that they think I am (*smart*) __the smartest__ person __in__ the class.

2. One of (*popular*) _____________________ holidays _____________________ Japan is New Year's.

3. A mouse is (*small*) _____________________ a rat.

4. Europe is first in agricultural production of potatoes. (*potatoes*) _____________________ are

   grown in Europe _____________________ on any other continent.

5. Mercury is (*close*) _____________________ planet to the sun. It moves around the sun (*fast*)

   _____________________ any other planet in the solar system.

6. In terms of area, (*large*) _____________________ state _____________________ the

   United States is Alaska, but it has one of (*small*) _____________________ populations

   _____________________ all the states.

7. I need more facts. I can't make my decision until I get (*information*) ___________________.

8. Rebecca is a wonderful person. I don't think I've ever met a (*kind*) ___________________ and
(*generous*) ___________________ person.

9. You can trust Rebecca. You will never meet a (*honest*) ___________________ person
___________________ she is.

10. I'm leaving. This is (*bad*) ___________________ movie I've ever seen! I won't sit through
another second of it.

11. One of (*safe*) ___________________ places to be during a lightning storm is inside a car.

12. Small birds have a much (*fast*) ___________________ heartbeat ___________________
large birds.

13. Are your feet exactly the same size? Almost everyone's left foot is (*big*) ___________________
their right foot.*

PRACTICE 26 ▸ *Like, alike.* (Chart 9-11)
Complete the sentences with ***like*** or ***alike***.

1. My mother and my father rarely argue because they think ___________ alike ___________.

2. The Browns designed their summer cabin to look ___________ like ___________ the inside of a boat.

3. Joe and John are twins, but they don't look ___________ alike ___________.

4. They dress ___________ alike ___________ because they have the same taste in clothes.

5. This lamp doesn't look ___________ like ___________ the one I ordered.

6. Mike is 30, but he acts ___________ like ___________ a child.

7. Professor Miller's lectures are all ___________ alike ___________: repetitive and boring.

8. This coffee doesn't taste ___________ like ___________ the coffee we sampled at the store.

9. The clouds in the east look ___________ like ___________ rain clouds.

10. My grandmother and mother sound ___________ alike ___________ on the phone.

PRACTICE 27 ▸ *The same, similar, different.* (Chart 9-11)
Complete the sentences with *the **same**, **similar***, or ***different*** and the correct preposition: ***as***,
to, or ***from***.

1. My coat is not like yours. It's ___________ different from ___________ yours.

2. Our apartment is a lot like my cousin's apartment. It's ___________________ hers.

3. The news report on Channel 4 at 7:00 P.M. was exactly ___________________ the report we
heard on Channel 6 at 6:00 P.M.

4. Is the North Pole really ___________________ the South Pole? I thought they were exactly alike.

5. Your jacket is just like mine. It's exactly ___________________ mine.

6. I enjoyed reading your letters from China. My experiences in Beijing were a lot like yours. They
were ___________________ yours in many ways.

---

*Grammar note: In formal English, a singular pronoun is used to refer to *everyone*:
    Everyone has **his or her** *own opinion.*
In everyday informal usage, a plural pronoun is frequently used:
    Everyone has **their** *own opinion.*

7. Except for some minor differences in grammar, spelling, and vocabulary, American English is

   ___________________________ British English. It's one language.

8. The English spoken in the United States is only slightly ___________________________ the English

   spoken in Britain, Canada, and Australia. The most noticeable difference is the accent.

9. Lemons are ___________________________ limes. They both taste sour.

10. My sisters are twins, but they are very ___________________________ each other. They don't even

    look alike.

PRACTICE 28 ▸ *Like, alike, similar, different.* (Chart 9-11)

Part I. Compare the figures using the given words.

1. like _______ *A is like D* _______.

2. alike ___________________________.

3. similar (to) ___________________________ and ___________________________.

4. different (from) ___________________________, ___________________________, and ___________________________.

Part II. Compare the figures. Use *the same (as)*, *similar (to)*, or *different (from)*.

5. All the triangles are ___________________________ each other.

6. A and D are ___________________________ each other.

7. A and C are ___________________________.

8. A isn't ___________________________ C.

9. B and C are ___________________________ D.

PRACTICE 29 ▸ *The same, similar, different, like, alike.* (Chart 9-11)

Complete the sentences with *the same*, *similar*, *different*, *like*, or *alike*.

1. Dana swims _______ *like* _______ a fish. She never wants to come out of the water.

2. The lake doesn't have a ripple on it. It looks ___________________________ glass.

3. There are six girls in our family, but none of us look _________________. Our brothers also look different.

4. A: Some people can tell we're sisters. Do you think we look _________________?

   B: Somewhat. The color of your hair is not _________________, but your eyes are exactly _________________ color. You also have _________________ oval face.

5. A: Excuse me. I believe you have my umbrella.

   B: Oh, you're right. It looks almost exactly _________________ mine, doesn't it?

6. A: This pasta is delicious! It tastes just _________________ the pasta we had in Italy.

   B: Well, not exactly. It's _________________ to the pasta in Italy, but it's not as good.

7. Some people think my sister and I are twins. We look _________________ and talk _________________, but our personalities are quite _________________.

8. Homonyms are words that have _________________ pronunciation but different spelling, such as "pair" and "pear" or "sea" and "see." For many people, "been" and "bean" are homonyms and have _________________ pronunciation. For other people, however, "been" and "bean" are words with _________________ pronunciations. These people pronounce "been" like "bin" or "ben."

PRACTICE 30 ▸ Check your knowledge. (Chapter 9 Review)

Correct the errors.

1. My brother is older ~~from~~ *than* me.

2. A sea is more deeper than a lake.

3. A donkey isn't as big to a horse.

4. Ellen is happiest person I've ever met.

5. When I feel embarrassed, my face gets hot and more hot.

6. One of a largest animal in the world is the hippopotamus.

7. The traffic on the highway is more bad than it used to be.

8. Jack is the same old as Jerry.

9. Peas are similar from beans, but they have several differences.

10. Last winter was pretty mild. This winter is cold and rainy. It's much rain than last winter.

11. Mrs. Peters, the substitute teacher, is very friendly than the regular instructor.

12. Although alligators and crocodiles are similar, alligators are less big than crocodiles.

13. Mohammed and Tarek come from different countries, but they became friends easily because they speak a same language, Arabic.

14. Leah and Kate are sisters. They look a lot like, but Leah is tallest than Leah.

15. Ramzy is an excellent student. He is the most good student in his class.

16. I ordered a new dress. I like it, but it doesn't look alike the picture online.

17. Abby wears a different pair of shoes every day. She owns more shoes anyone I know.

18. San Francisco is a very windy city. Is it windy as Chicago?

PRACTICE 31 ▶ Crossword puzzle. (Chapter 9 Review)
Complete the crossword puzzle. Use the clues to find the correct words.

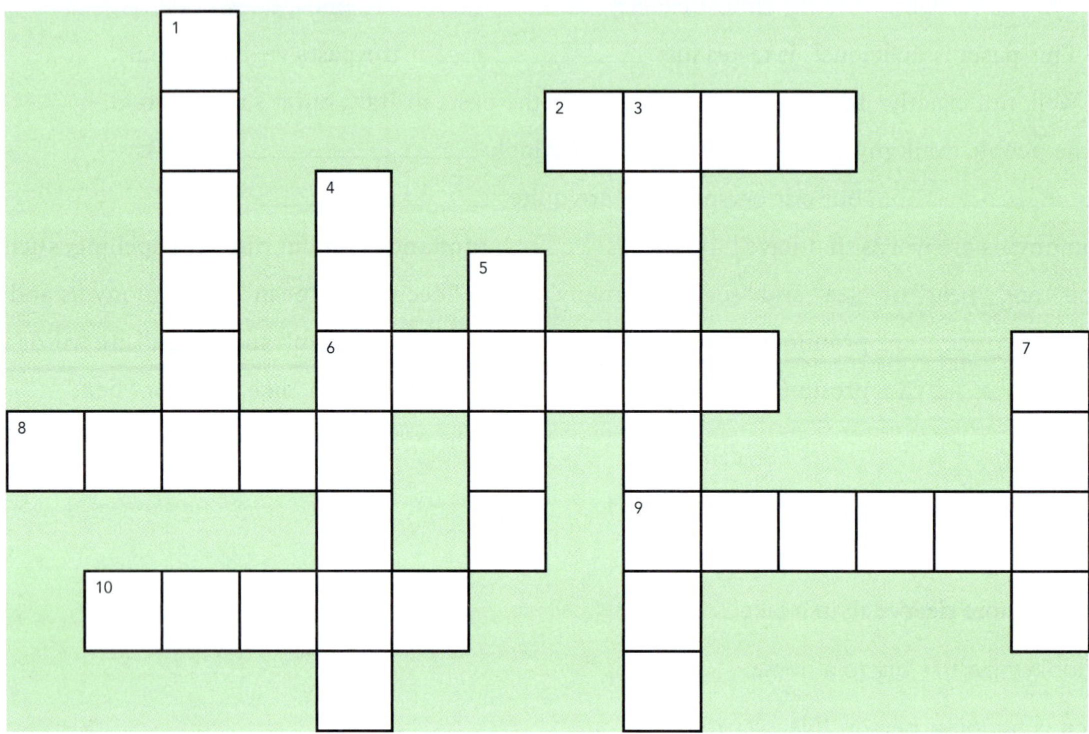

Across

2. My husband is a good cook, but my mother is the _______________ cook in the world.

6. A turtle walks more _______________ than a rabbit.

8. The weather is really bad this summer. It rains all the time, and the heat is terrible. It's the _______________ summer we've ever had.

9. Arithmetic is _______________ than advanced calculus.

10. I have a bad cold. I went to work, but that was a mistake. I had to go home early. I feel even _______________ than I did this morning.

Down

1. Kim speaks English much _______________ than he did last year.

3. We are taking the _______________ plane tomorrow morning. It leaves at 6:00 A.M.

4. The _______________ swimmer won first prize.

5. Many people think that Paris is the _______________ beautiful city in the world.

7. There are _______________ letters in the word *happy* than in the word *sad*.

The Passive

PRACTICE 1 ▶ Active vs. passive. (Chart 10-1)
Circle "active" if the given sentence is active; circle "passive" if it is passive. <u>Underline</u> the verb.

1. (active)   passive   The janitor <u>cleans</u> the office every day.
2. active   (passive)   The office <u>is cleaned</u> by the janitor every day.
3. active   passive   Sara posted a comment.
4. active   passive   A comment was posted by Sara.
5. active   passive   The teacher explained the lesson.
6. active   passive   The lesson was explained by the teacher.
7. active   passive   Bridges are designed by engineers.
8. active   passive   Engineers design bridges.
9. active   passive   The mechanic is fixing my car.
10. active   passive   My car is being fixed right now.

PRACTICE 2 ▶ Active vs. passive. (Charts 10-1 and 10-2)
Change the active verbs in *italics* to passive.

1. Mr. Case *delivers* our mail every day.   Our mail _____ *is delivered* _____ by Mr. Case every day.

2. Mr. Case *delivered* our mail early today.   Our mail _____ was delivered _____ by Mr. Case early today.

3. Mr. Case *has delivered* our mail for years.   Our mail _____ has been delivered _____ by Mr. Case for years.

4. Mr. Case *is going to deliver* our mail late today.   Our mail _____ is being delivered _____ by Mr. Case late today.

5. Mr. Case *will deliver* the mail early on Saturday.   Our mail _____ will be delivered _____ by Mr. Case early on Saturday.

Write the past participles of the given verbs. The list contains both regular and irregular verbs.

1. bring _____*brought*_____
2. build _______________
3. buy _______________
4. carry _______________
5. do _______________
6. eat _______________
7. feed _______________
8. find _______________
9. give _______________
10. go _______________
11. grow _______________
12. hit _______________
13. hurt _______________
14. invite _______________
15. leave _______________

16. lose _______________
17. make _______________
18. plan _______________
19. play _______________
20. pull _______________
21. read _______________
22. save _______________
23. send _______________
24. speak _______________
25. spend _______________
26. take _______________
27. teach _______________
28. visit _______________
29. wear _______________
30. write _______________

PRACTICE 4 ▸ Forming the passive. (Chart 10-2)

Complete the sentences with the given form of *be* and the past participle of any appropriate verbs in the list in Practice 3.

1. *is* Arabic _____*is spoken*_____ by more than 800 million people.

2. *are* Books _______________ by authors.

3. *are* Books _______________ by readers.

4. *was* A new school _______________ in our town last year.

5. *were* The two lost children _______________ at the ice cream shop.

6. *has been* There's no more pizza. All the pizza _______________ by the kids.

7. *is going to be* Niagara Falls _______________ by thousands of tourists this year.

8. *will be* The championship football game _______________ in Milan next week.

9. *are going to be* Our pictures _______________ by a professional photographer at the wedding.

10. *have been* Oranges _______________ by farmers in Jordan since ancient times.

11. *haven't been* The dogs are very hungry. They _______________ yet today.

12. *weren't* We didn't go to the party because we _______________.

PRACTICE 5 ▸ Forming the passive. (Chart 10-2)

Complete the sentences with the passive form of the verbs in parentheses.

Use the <u>simple present</u>.

1. Coffee (*grow*) _____*is grown*_____ in hot climates.

2. Planes (*fly*)_______________ by pilots.

3. Armies (*lead*)_______________ by generals.

4. The month of May (*follow*)_______________ by the month of June.

Use the simple past.

5. I (*bite*) ______*was bitten*______ by a mosquito.

6. This video (*shoot*) ____________________ by our class.

7. These cookies (*make*) ____________________ by my grandmother.

8. Penicillin (*discover*) ____________________ by Alexander Fleming, a Scottish scientist.

Use the present perfect.

9. I (*invite*) ______*have been invited*______ to a special conference by the governor.

10. A book about our town (*write*) ____________________ by my sociology professor.

11. The house next to ours (*buy*) ____________________ by an airline pilot.

12. Two men (*arrest*) ____________________ by the police for robbing the bank last month.

Use the future (*will*).

13. We (*give*) ______*will be given*______ a tour of the new museum.

14. The wedding photos (*take*) ____________________ by a professional photographer.

15. A new president and vice-president (*elect*) ____________________ by the people.

16. The gold medal (*won*) ____________________ by the fastest runner.

Use the future (*be going to*).

17. The old hospital (*tear*) ______*is going to be torn*______ down.

18. The children (*teach*) ____________________ French by a native French speaker.

19. Five new employees (*hire*) ____________________ this month.

20. Your package (*send*) ____________________ by overnight mail. You'll receive it tomorrow.

PRACTICE 6 ▸ Tense forms of the passive. (Chart 10-2)

Complete the sentences with the passive form of the verbs in the boxes.

Part I. **Use the simple present.**

✓collect	grow	understand
eat	pay	write

1. Taxes ______*are collected*______ by the government.

2. Many textbooks ___are written___ by teachers.

3. Rice ___is grown___ by farmers in Korea.

4. Worms ___are eaten___ by birds.

5. I ___am paid___ for my work by my employer.

6. The meaning of a smile ___is understood___ by everyone.

Part II. **Use the simple past.**

build	✓collect	destroy	write

7. Yesterday the students' papers ______*were collected*______ by the teacher at the end of the test.

8. The Great Wall of China ___was built___ by Chinese emperors more than 2,500 years ago.

9. The *Harry Potter* books ___were written___ by J. K. Rowling, a former English teacher.

10. An office building in Jakarta ___was destroyed___ by the earthquake.

Part III. Use the **present perfect**.

read	speak	✓visit	wear

11. The pyramids in Egypt ______*have been visited*______ by millions of tourists.
12. Spanish _has been spoken_ by people in Latin America for centuries.
13. *War and Peace* is a famous book. It _has been read_ by millions of people.
14. Perfume _has been worn_ by both men and women since ancient times.

Part IV. Use the **future** (*will*).

✓discover	save	visit

15. New information about the universe ______*will be discovered*______ by scientists during this century.
16. Hawaii _will be visited_ by thousands of tourists this year.
17. Pandas _will be saved_ from extinction by the Chinese government and organizations like the World Wildlife Federation.

Part V. Use the **future** (a form of *be going to*).

choose	✓hurt	offer

18. Your friend ______*is going to be hurt*______ by your unkind remark when she hears about it.
19. New computer courses _is going to be chosen_ by the university next year.
20. The winner of the essay contest _is_ by the English teachers at our school.

PRACTICE 7 ▸ Passive vs. active meaning. (Charts 10-1 and 10-2)
Choose the sentence that has the same meaning as the given sentence.

1. My grandmother makes her own bread. Have a slice.

    a. This bread is made by my grandmother.

    b. Someone makes my grandmother's bread.

2. Bob was taken to the hospital by car.

    a. Bob drove to the hospital.

    b. Someone drove Bob to the hospital.

3. Suzanne has just been offered her first job.

    a. Suzanne has offered someone a job.

    b. Someone has offered Suzanne a job.

4. You will be informed of the test results.

    a. Someone will inform you of the test results.

    b. You will inform someone of the test results.

5. A sign: "You are not allowed to enter."

    a. You do not allow people to enter.

    b. Someone says you cannot enter.

6. The child was saved after five minutes in the water.

    a. Someone saved the child.

    b. The child saved herself.

7. An announcement on the phone: "For security purposes, this conversation is being recorded."

    a. You are recording the conversation.

    b. Someone else is recording the conversation.

PRACTICE 8 ▸ Passive to active. (Charts 10-1 and 10-2)

Change the passive sentences to active. Keep the same tense of each sentence. Some of the sentences are questions.

1. A new film from India, *Falling Rocks*, will be shown by the City Film Society.
   The City Film Society will show a new film from India, Falling Rocks.

2. The film has been reviewed by movie critics.
   ____

3. The movie was given good ratings by audiences.
   ____

4. Was the movie written by a famous writer?
   ____

5. The lead role is played by an unknown actor.
   ____

6. Is a murder committed by someone in the movie?
   ____

7. Is the main character killed by a spy?
   ____

8. Will the movie be seen by many people?
   ____

9. Is an award going to be won by the movie?
   ____

PRACTICE 9 ▸ Progressive forms of the passive. (Chart 10-3)

Change the active verbs to passive.

Yesterday was a very busy day at the office.

1. Someone was repairing the printer.

   The printer ______ *was being repaired* ______.

2. The managers were holding a meeting in the conference room.

   A meeting _______________________ in the conference room.

3. The secretary was taking notes at the meeting.

   Notes _______________________ at the meeting.

Today is another busy day.

4. Someone is using the copier right now.

   The copier _________________________________ right now.

5. I am ordering office supplies.

   Office supplies _________________________________.

6. The receptionist is answering calls.

   Calls _________________________________.

PRACTICE 10 ▸ Progressive forms of the passive. (Chart 10-3)

Change the sentences from active to passive. Do not include the subject of the active sentence.

I had to take my car to the mechanic's yesterday. While I was waiting at a nearby café …

1. A mechanic was inspecting the brakes.
   The brakes were being inspected.

2. Another was changing the oil.

   ____

3. He also checked the tire pressure.

   ____

4. He added windshield wiper fluid.

   ____

The mechanic found some problems. Today …

5. He is installing new brake pads.

   ____

6. He is replacing a broken headlight.

   ____

7. He is repairing the transmission.

   ____

8. He is balancing and rotating the tires.

   ____

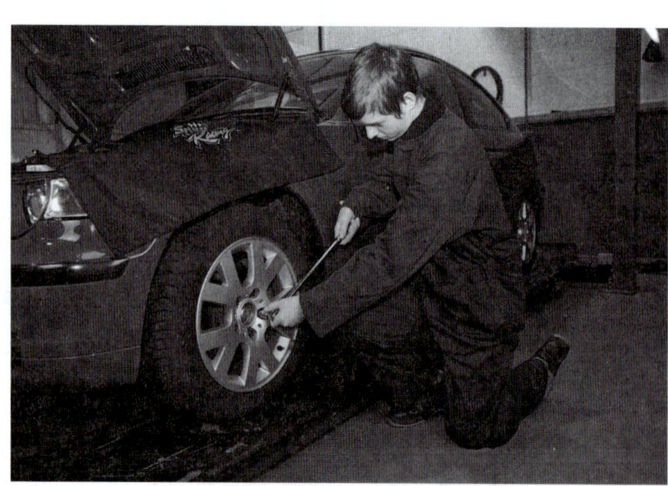

Change the questions from active to passive.

1. Did many people see the game?

   Was the game seen by many people?

2. Will the news shock Pat?

3. Is the restaurant serving lunch now?

4. Does everyone understand the rules?

5. Is the professor going to explain the solution?

6. Has the university accepted you?

7. Have both the seller and the buyer signed the contract?

8. Did the police find the suspect?

9. Is someone helping you?

10. Has the mail carrier delivered the packages yet?

PRACTICE 12 ▸ Transitive vs. intransitive. (Chart 10-4)

Circle "transitive" if the verb takes an object. Circle "intransitive" if it does not. <u>Underline</u> the object of the verb.

1. transitive   intransitive   Alex wrote <u>an email</u>.
2. transitive   intransitive   Alex wrote to his parents. (*There is no object of the verb.*)
3. transitive   intransitive   Rita bought groceries.
4. transitive   intransitive   Sam walked to his office.
5. transitive   intransitive   Kate threw the ball.
6. transitive   intransitive   My plane arrived at six-thirty.
7. transitive   intransitive   Emily is crying.
8. transitive   intransitive   Our cat caught a snake.
9. transitive   intransitive   Someone returned the book to the library.
10. transitive   intransitive   A strange light appeared in the sky last night.
11. transitive   intransitive   I slept late this morning.
12. transitive   intransitive   Jeff left his keys in the office.

PRACTICE 13 ▸ Active and passive. (Charts 10-1 → 10-4)

<u>Underline</u> the object of the verb if the sentence has one. Then change the sentence to the passive if possible.

Active	Passive
1. It was raining hard last night.	_No change._
2. Around midnight, loud sounds awakened <u>me</u>.	_I was awakened by loud sounds around midnight._
3. Lightning struck a tree.	
4. The tree fell down.	
5. The tree hit my neighbor's car.	
6. The impact set off the car alarm.	
7. The car alarm sounded very loud.	
8. The tree damaged the roof of the car.	
9. Fortunately, no one was inside the car.	

PRACTICE 14 ▸ Review: identifying passives with transitive and intransitive verbs.
(Charts 10-1 → 10-4)

Check (✓) the sentences that are passive.

1. _________ I came by plane.
2. ___✓___ I was invited to the party by Alex.
3. _________ Many people died during the earthquake.
4. _________ Many people were killed by collapsing buildings.
5. _________ The earthquake has killed many people.
6. _________ The game will be won by the home team.
7. _________ The home team will win the game.
8. _________ Gina's baby cried for more than an hour.
9. _________ Most of the fresh fruit at the market was bought by customers.
10. _________ Some customers bought boxes full of fresh fruit.
11. _________ Accidents always occur at that intersection.

PRACTICE 15 ▸ The *by*-phrase. (Chart 10-5)

<u>Underline</u> the passive verbs. Answer the questions. If you don't know the exact person or people who performed the action, write **unknown**.

1. Soft duck feathers <u>are used</u> to make pillows.

   Who uses duck feathers to make pillows? _______ unknown _______

2. The mail <u>was opened</u> by Shelley.

   Who opened the mail? _______ Shelley _______

3. Eric Wong's new book will be translated into many languages.

   Who will translate Eric Wong's new book? ________________________

4. Rebecca's bike was stolen yesterday from in front of the library.

   Who stole Rebecca's bike? _______________

5. The Warren's house was designed by a famous architect.

   Who designed the Warren's house? _______________

6. Malawi is a small country in southeastern Africa. A new highway is going to be built in Malawi next year.

   Who is going to build the new highway? _______________

7. There are no more empty apartments in our building. The apartment next to ours has been rented by a young family with two small children.

   Who rented the apartment next to ours? _______________

8. The apartment directly above ours was empty for two months, but now it has also been rented.

   Who rented the apartment directly above ours? _______________

PRACTICE 16 ▸ Active to passive. (Charts 10-1 → 10-5)

Change the active sentences to passive. Use the **by**-phrase only if necessary.

1. Someone has canceled the soccer game.

   The soccer game has been canceled. _______________

2. The president has canceled the meeting.

   The meeting has been canceled by the president. _______________

3. Someone serves ethnic dishes at that restaurant.

   ____

4. Something confused me in class yesterday.

   ____

5. The teacher's directions confused me.

   ____

6. No one has washed the dishes yet.

   ____

7. Someone will wash them soon.

   ____

8. Did someone wash this sweater in hot water?

   ____

9. Luis invited me to the party.

   ____

10. Has anyone invited you to the party?

   ____

Make sentences with the given words. Use the present tense. Some are passive and some are not. Do not change the word order.

1. Sometimes keys \ hide \ under cars

   Sometimes keys are hidden under cars.

2. Cats \ hide \ under cars

   Cats hide under cars.

3. Students \ teach \ by teachers

   ____

4. Students \ study \ a lot

   ____

5. Cereal \ often eat \ at breakfast

   ____

6. Kate \ feed \ the cat \ every day.

   ____

7. The cat \ feed \ by Kate \ every day.

   ____

8. Songs \ sing \ to children \ by their mothers

   ____

9. Thai food \ cook \ in Thai restaurants

   ____

10. Chefs \ cook \ in restaurants

    ____

PRACTICE 18 ▸ Meaning of passive verbs. (Charts 10-1 → 10-5)

Choose the sentence that has the same meaning as the given sentence.

1. A mouse is being chased.

   a. A mouse is trying to catch something.

   b. Something is trying to catch a mouse.

2. The mouse was caught.

   a. The mouse caught something.

   b. Something caught the mouse.

3. The soldiers are being trained.

   a. Someone is training the soldiers.

   b. The soldiers are training someone.

4. The earthquake victims are being helped by the medics.

   a. The medics are receiving help.

   b. The victims are receiving help.

5. Some pets are taught to do tricks.

   a. Some pets teach themselves to do tricks.

   b. Someone teaches the pets to do tricks.

6. The children were trying to find their parents after the school play.

   a. The children were looking for their parents.

   b. The parents were looking for their children.

7. The airline passengers were being asked to wait while the plane was cleaned.

   a. The passengers made a request.

   b. Someone asked the passengers to wait.

8. The flight attendants were instructed to be seated.

   a. Someone told the flight attendants to be seated.

   b. The flight attendants told people to be seated.

PRACTICE 19 ▸ **Review: active vs. passive.** (Charts 10-1 → 10-5)
Write "C" if the sentence is correct and "I" if incorrect. Make any necessary corrections.

1. ___*I*___ It ~~was~~ happened many years ago.

2. ___C___ Wheat is grown in Canada.

3. _______ I was go to school yesterday.

4. _______ Two firefighters injure while they were fighting the fire.

5. _______ Sara was accidentally broken the window.

6. _______ Kara was eating a snack when her phone rang.

7. _______ Tim was eaten when his phone rang.

8. _______ I am agree with you.

9. _______ The little boy was fallen down while he was running in the park.

10. _______ The swimmer was died from a shark attack.

11. _______ The swimmer was killed by a shark.

12. _______ I was slept for nine hours last night.

PRACTICE 20 ▸ **Passive modals.** (Chart 10-6)
Complete the sentences by changing the active modals to passive modals.

1. This book (*have to return*) _____*has to be returned*_____ to the library today.

2. That book (*should return*) _____________________ tomorrow.

3. This bill (*must pay*) _____________________ today.

4. This package (*could send*) _____________________ tomorrow.

5. That package (*should send*) _____________________ by overnight mail.

6. That box (*can put away*) _____________________ now.

7. These boxes (*may throw away*) _____________________ soon.

8. Those boxes (*might pick up*) _____________________ this afternoon.

9. This room (*will clean up*) _____________________ soon.

Change the answers from active to passive. Include the **by**-phrase only if it contains important information.

1. *What happens when an animal is sick?*

   a. A veterinarian should treat the animal.

   The animal should be treated by a veterinarian.

   b. Someone will give the animal medicine.

   The animal will be given medicine.

2. *Can I send this letter now?*

   a. No, someone has to change the last paragraph.

   ____

   b. No, Mr. Hayes must sign it.

   ____

3. *What's going to happen to that big old house on Maple Street?*

   a. A famous hockey star might buy it.

   ____

   b. Someone may turn it into apartments.

   ____

4. *There's a mistake on my credit card bill.*

   a. You should call the credit card company immediately.

   ____

   b. The company ought to fix the mistake right away.

   ____

5. *There's a new book about everyday heroes.*

   a. Everyone should read it.

   ____

   b. They will make a movie of the book.

   ____

6. *This dress is too long for me.*

   a. Someone should shorten it.

   ____

   b. Someone has to do it soon.

   ____

7. *Someone stole my wallet.*

   a. You should report it to the police.

   ____

   b. You have to cancel your credit cards.

   ____

Choose the correct completions.

Telling Time

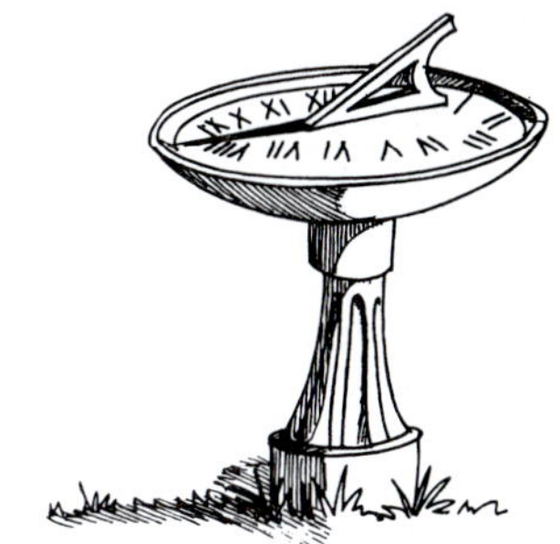

(1) Sundials   used / ~~were used~~   in ancient times to tell time. Clocks first   appeared / were appeared   during the 13th century. The first watches   made / were made   in Europe six hundred years ago. These watches   worn / were worn   around a person's neck. In the 1600s, men   began / were begun   to put the watches inside their pockets. These watches   called / were called   pocket watches. The watches   became / were become   popular and   were remained / remained   popular until World War I. During that war, watches   put / were put   on bands, and soldiers   wore / were worn   the bands around their wrists. It was more practical to look quickly at a watch on the wrist than to pull a watch out of a pocket. Since then, millions of wristwatches   have been manufactured / have manufactured.

(2) In the early 2000s, not as many watches   were being sold / sold   as they were previously. This was because many people   checked / were checked   the time on their computers, tablets, and cell phones. Watches   weren't needed / didn't need   as much as they had been before. Some people thought that the need for wristwatches   might disappear / might be disappeared   completely. They wondered if wristwatches   could be considered / could consider   an antique item, like the pocket watch.

(3) Today, watches have   become / have been become   very popular once again. However, the traditional wristwatch   is replacing / is being replaced   by the smartwatch. Smartwatches   feature / are featured   a touchscreen and   offer / are offered   far more functions than a traditional wristwatch. Smartwatch wearers   can use / can be used   their watch to make phone calls. Apps   can download / can be downloaded,   and they   can manage / can be managed   on a smartwatch. Most models also   include / are included   a GPS and a fitness tracker. Smartwatches   design / are designed   to function as both a watch and a phone.

PRACTICE 23 ▸ Using past participles as adjectives. (Chart 10-7)

Complete the sentences with the correct prepositions.

Part I. Jack is …

1. married ______*to*______ Katie.

2. excited ______________ vacation.

3. exhausted ______________ work.

4. frightened ______________ heights.

5. disappointed ______________ his new car.

6. tired ______________ rain.

7. pleased ______________ his new boss.

8. involved ______________ charity work.

9. worried ______________ his elderly parents.

10. acquainted ______________ a famous movie star.

Part II. Jack's friend is …

11. interested _____________ sports.

12. done _____________ final exams.

13. terrified _____________ spiders.

14. related _____________ a famous movie star.

15. opposed _____________ gun ownership.

16. pleased _____________ his part-time job.

17. divorced _____________ his wife.

Part III. Jack's house is …

18. made _____________ wood.

19. located _____________ the suburbs.

20. crowded _____________ antique furniture.

21. prepared _____________ emergencies.

PRACTICE 24 ▸ Using past participles as adjectives. (Chart 10-7)

Correct the errors.

1. The little girl is ~~excite in~~ *excited about* her birthday party.

2. Mr. and Mrs. Rose devoted each other.

3. Could you please help me? I need directions. I lost.

4. The students are boring in their chemistry project.

5. The paper bags at this store is composed in recycled products.

6. Your friend needs a doctor. He hurt.

7. How well are you prepare the driver's license test?

8. Mary has been engage with Paul for five years. Will they ever get married?

PRACTICE 25 ▸ -*ed* vs. -*ing*. (Chart 10-8)

Complete the sentences with the appropriate **-*ed*** or **-*ing*** form of the words in parentheses.

Ben is reading a book. He really likes it. He can't put it down. He has to keep reading.

1. The book is really ____*interesting*____. (*interest*)

2. Ben is really _____________. (*interest*)

3. The story is _____________. (*excite*)

4. Ben is _____________ about the story. (*excite*)

5. Ben is _____________ by the characters in the book. (*fascinate*)

6. The people in the story are _____________. (*fascinate*)

7. Ben didn't finish the last book he started because it was _____________ and
_____________. (*bore, confuse*)

8. Ben doesn't like to read books when he is _____________ and
_____________. (*bore, confuse*)

9. What is the most _________ *interesting* _________ book you've read lately? (*interest*)

10. I just finished a _________ *fascinated* _________ mystery story that had a very

    _________________________ ending. (*fascinate, surprise*)

PRACTICE 26 ▶ *-ed* vs. *-ing.* (Chart 10-8)

Choose the correct completions.

1. The students are   interesting / interested   in learning more about Kung Fu.

2. Ms. Green doesn't explain things well. She's   confusing / confused.

    The students are   confusing / confused.

3. Have you heard the news about Jamie and Hal? They are going trekking in Nepal. They are

    really   exciting / excited   about it. It's really an   exciting / excited   thing to do.

4. There was a   surprising / surprised   event in the news yesterday: The governor had resigned

    suddenly. Everyone was   surprising / surprised.

5. It's   embarrassing / embarrassed   to forget someone's name. Yesterday, I couldn't remember

    the name of my manager's wife, and I felt very   embarrassed / embarrassing.

6. Mr. Ball fascinates me. He has lived in 13 countries and he speaks five languages. I think he is

    a   fascinating / fascinated   person. Whenever I am with him, I listen to everything he says.

    I am   fascinating / fascinated   by Mr. Ball.

PRACTICE 27 ▶ *-ed* vs. *-ing.* (Chart 10-8)

Write "I" next to the incorrect sentence in each group.

1. a. _____ Science fascinates me.

   b. _____ Science is fascinating to me.

   c. __I__ Science is fascinated to me.

2. a. _____ The baby is exciting about her new toy.

   b. _____ The baby is excited about her new toy.

   c. _____ The new toy is exciting to the baby.

3. a. _____ The book is really interesting.

   b. _____ The book is really interested.

   c. _____ The book interests me.

4. a. _____ I am exhausting from working 60-hour weeks.

   b. _____ I am exhausted from working 60-hour weeks.

   c. _____ Working 60-hour weeks exhausts me.

   d. _____ Working 60-hour weeks is exhausting.

5. a. _____ Your grandmother is amazing to me.

   b. _____ Your grandmother amazes me.

   c. _____ Your grandmother is amazed to me.

   d. _____ I am amazed by your grandmother.

Complete the sentences with the correct *–ed* or *–ing* adjective of the word in parentheses.

1. Sophie was very (*embarrass*) _____*embarrassed*_____ by all the attention she got for her high test scores.

2. Sophie said it was (*embarrass*) _____________________ to have so many people congratulate her.

3. I am really (*interest*) _____________________ in eighteenth-century art.

4. Eighteenth-century art is really (*interest*) _____________________.

5. What an (*exhaust*) _____________________ day! I am so _____________________ (*tire*) from picking strawberries.

6. Working outside in the hot sun is (*exhaust*) _____________________.

7. Some of the new horror movies are (*frighten*) _____________________ because they are so realistic.

8. If young children see a horror movie, they often become (*frighten*) _____________________ and have bad dreams.

9. The street signs in our city are (*confuse*) _____________________.

10. The drivers are (*confuse*) _____________________ and (*frustrate*) _____________________ by all the signs.

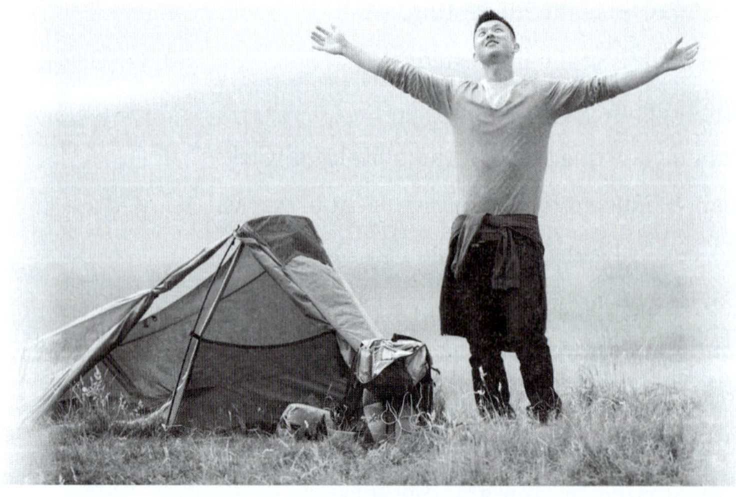

Choose the correct answers.

1. We couldn't go on our vacation to Hawaii because we got _____ with the flu.   a. dressed

2. Jerry couldn't find our house. He got _____ on the way.   b. late

3. Susie is five years old now. She can get _____ by herself.   c. lost

4. When's dinner going to be ready? I'm getting very _____.   d. caught

5. We'll be late for the concert if we don't hurry. It's getting _____.   e. wet

6. I want to make a lot of money. Do you know a good way to get _____ quick?   f. rich

7. Jake is on academic probation. He got _____ cheating on a test.   g. sick

8. Last Saturday I went camping. I was setting up our tent when it suddenly   h. hungry
started to rain. I got very _____.

PRACTICE 30 ▸ Get + adjective and past participle. (Chart 10-9)

Complete the sentences with an appropriate form of *get*.

1. Hurry up! _______*Get*_______ busy. There's no time to waste.

2. Tom and Sue _______*got*_______ married last month.

3. Let's stop working for a while. I _______________ tired.

4. I _______________ interested in biology when I was in high school, so I decided to major in it in college.

5. When I was in the hospital, I got a card from my aunt and uncle. It said, "_______________ well soon."

6. Karen used to _______________ lost all the time, but now she always uses GPS.

7. A: What happened to you just now?

   B: I don't know. Suddenly I _______________ dizzy, but I'm okay now.

8. I always _______________ nervous when I have to give a speech.

9. A: Where's Brad? He was supposed to be home two hours ago. He always calls when he's late.

   I _______________ worried. Maybe we should call the police.

   B: Relax. He'll be home soon

10. A: I'm going on a diet.

    B: Oh?

    A: See? This shirt is too tight. I _______________ fat.

PRACTICE 31 ▸ Be used / accustomed to. (Chart 10-10)

Choose the correct answers. More than one answer may be correct.

1. Frank has lived alone for 20 years. He _____ alone.

   a. used to live   b. is used to living   c. is accustomed to living

2. I _____ with my family, but now I live alone.

   a. used to live   b. am used to living   c. am accustomed to living

3. Rita rides her bike to work every day. She _____ her bike to work.

   a. used to ride   b. is used to riding   c. is accustomed to riding

4. Thomas rode his bike to work for many years, but now he takes the bus. Tom _____ his bike to work.

   a. used to ride   b. is used to riding   c. is accustomed to riding

5. Carl _____ to work, but now he takes a train.

   a. used to drive   b. is used to driving   c. is accustomed to driving

6. Carl drives 50 miles to work every day. He _____ 50 miles a day.

   a. used to drive   b. is used to driving   c. is accustomed to driving

7. Ari _____ dinner at 9:00 P.M. He has dinner at that time every night. That's too late for me.

   a. used to eat   b. is used to eating   c. is accustomed to eating

8. Maria _____ dinner at 9:00 P.M., but now she eats at 6:00 P.M. with her roommates.

   a. used to eat   b. is used to eating   c. is accustomed to eating

Add an appropriate form of *be* if necessary. If no form of *be* is needed, write **Ø**.

1. People ___Ø___ used to take trains to travel long distances, but today most people take airplanes.

2. Polly Hudson often has to travel for her job. She ___*is*___ used to traveling by plane.

3. You and I are from different cultures. You _______ used to having fish for breakfast. I _______ used to having cheese and bread for breakfast.

4. When I lived at home, I _______ used to have big breakfasts. Now I am living in an apartment on my own, and I don't eat breakfast anymore.

5. Jeremy wakes up at 5:00 every morning for work. After a year of doing this, he _______ used to getting up early, even on weekends.

6. Our neighbor, Dr. Jenkins, retired last year. He _______ used to get up early to go to work at the hospital, but now he gets up whenever he wants.

7. Before email, people _______ used to write letters. Letters are less common nowadays.

8. My grandfather doesn't use the computer much. He _______ used to talking on the phone. When he wants to communicate with us, he phones us.

9. Minna Lee has been our senator for several years. She has never lost an election. She _______ used to winning elections.

10. Sam Sibley _______ used to be our senator. He was our senator for 26 years until he died at age 87.

Complete the sentences with *used to* or *be used to* and the correct form of the verb in parentheses.

1. Kate grew up on a farm. She (*get*) _____*used to get*_____ up at dawn and go to bed as soon as the sun went down. Now she works in the city at an advertising agency and has different sleeping hours.

2. Hiroki's workweek is seven days long. He (*work*) _________________________ on Saturdays and Sundays.

3. Luis spends weekends with his family now. He (*play*) _________________ soccer on a team before he was married, but now he enjoys staying home with his young children.

4. Sally (*be*) _________________ a nurse. But six years ago, she applied to medical school and was accepted. Now she is a doctor.

5. Joan has taught kindergarten for eight years. She is very patient with small children. She (*work*) _________________________ with them.

6. Bebo really likes hot and spicy food. He always orders it in a restaurant. He (*eat*) _________________________ hot and spicy food, and he never orders anything else.

Make sentences with a similar meaning by using a form of *be supposed to.*

1. Someone expected me to return this book to the library yesterday, but I didn't.
   I was supposed to return this book to the library.

2. Our professor expects us to read Chapter 9 before class tomorrow.
   We are supposed to read chapter 9.

3. Someone expected me to go to a party last night, but I stayed home.
   I was supposed to go a

4. The teacher expects us to do Exercise 10 for homework.

We are supposed to do it.

5. The weather channel has predicted rain for tomorrow.

Rain has be supposed for tomorrow by the weather channel.
It is supposed rain Tomorrow

6. The directions on the medicine bottle say, "Take one pill every six hours."

I was said "~" by the directions on the medicine bottle.

7. My mother expects me to dust the furniture and vacuum the carpet.

I am supposed to dust the furniture and vacuum the carpet.

PRACTICE 35 ▸ Check your knowledge. (Chapter 10 Review)

Correct the errors.

1. The moving boxes^were packed by Pierre.

2. Miami located in Florida.

3. I was very worry about my son.

4. Mr. Rivera interested in finding a new career.

5. Did you tell everyone the shocked news?

6. After ten years, I finally used to this wet and rainy climate.

7. The Millers have been marry with each other for 60 years.

8. I am use to drink coffee with cream, but now I drink it black*.

9. A new parking garage being build for our office.

10. I have been living in England for several years, so I accustom driving on the left side of the road.

PRACTICE 36 ▸ Active and passive verbs. (Chapter 10 Review)

Choose the correct completions.

Our town   *hit / was hit*   by a hurricane a few months ago. We live near the coast, so we   *used to / are used to*   hurricanes, but this one was especially bad.   Our house *destroyed / was destroyed*.   The roof   *tore off / was torn off*   during the storm, and a tree   *fell / was fallen*   through a window. We   *lost / were lost*   most of our belongings, but we   *feel / were felt*   very lucky because we weren't   *injured / injuring*   during the storm.   We *left / were left*   the night before the hurricane. We stayed with our kind and   *cared / caring*   friends. Fortunately, our house   *insured / was insured*.   Now, our house is   *being / been*   fixed. The roof and windows *are replacing / are being replaced*. The work *should complete / should be completed* soon. We *suppose to / are supposed to* move back into our house next month.

---

black = without cream.

PRACTICE 1 ▶ *A* vs. *an*: singular count nouns. (Chart 11-1)
Write *a* or *an*.

1. _____*a*_____ game
2. _________ office
3. _________ car
4. _________ egg
5. _________ man
6. _________ university
7. _________ umbrella
8. _________ house
9. _________ island
10. _________ ocean
11. _________ hour
12. _________ horse
13. _________ star

14. _________ eye
15. _________ new game
16. _________ large office
17. _________ old car
18. _________ used car
19. _________ honest man
20. _________ large university
21. _________ small house
22. _________ empty house
23. _________ green apple
24. _________ interesting book
25. _________ news article
26. _________ history teacher

PRACTICE 2 ▶ Count and noncount nouns. (Chart 11-2)
Choose the correct completions.

1. Sal is sitting in   chair / a chair.
2. There are four   chair / chairs   at the table.
3. There are some   chair / chairs   near the wall.
4. One   chair / chairs   is broken.
5. I like the   furniture / furnitures   in this room.
6. Some / A   furniture in this room came from Italy.
7. Furniture / A furniture   can be expensive.
8. Tomorrow we are going to buy   one / some   furniture.
9. Sal needs a new   desk / desks.
10. He looked at some   desk / desks   last week, but they weren't the right size.

PRACTICE 3 ▸ Noncount nouns. (Chart 11-3)
Write the words in their correct categories.

✓apples   bracelets   necklaces   sofas
backpacks   chairs   oranges   strawberries
bananas   earrings   purses   suitcases
beds   ✓handbags   rings   tables

Baggage	Fruit	Jewelry	Furniture
handbags	*apples*		

PRACTICE 4 ▸ More noncount nouns. (Chart 11-4)
Complete the sentences with the correct words from the box.

fun   gold   help   light   thunder   water

1. Sally drank some ________________.
2. It's too dark in here. We need some ________________.
3. Listen! Is that ________________?
4. These rings are made of ________________.
5. I need some ________________. Can you please carry this package for me?
6. It was a great party. Everybody had ________________.

PRACTICE 5 ▸ Count and noncount nouns. (Charts 11-1 → 11-4)
Complete the sentences with *-s/-es* or Ø if nothing should be added.

1. Would you please pass the salt ______ and pepper ______?
2. It's very cold here, and there's been a lot of snow ______. You'll need to bring your warm
   boot ______ and a heavy jacket. And don't forget wool sock ______.
3. Dad made some cookie ______ for the children to have with their milk ______.
4. I wasn't hungry for lunch. I just had some soup ______, and some bread ______ and
   butter ______.
5. Pat slipped on the ice ______ and broke two bone ______ in his foot.
6. There has been rain ______ all week. I'd like to see some sunshine ______ soon.
7. Teachers need patience ______ with their students. The teachers are satisfied when the students
   make progress ______.

Complete the sentences with **a/an** or **Ø**.

1. Tom lived in __*a*__ big city for many years. However, three years ago he left the city. It had __Ø__
   pollution and _____ smog, and he couldn't breathe well. Now he lives in _____ small town in the
   mountains. He breathes _____ clean air and drinks _____ fresh water. He knows that it was _____
   good idea to leave the city because his health is better.

2. Cornell University is named for Ezra Cornell. Ezra Cornell was a philanthropist* who lived in
   Ithaca, New York. He loved the area and wanted to improve it. People there didn't have _____
   library, and so he built one for them. Then he wanted to build _____ university where people
   could gain _____ knowledge in _____ practical subjects, such as farming, as well as in _____ history,
   _____ literature, and _____ science. Cornell owned _____ large farm in the area, and in an act of
   generosity, he donated it as the site for the new university. Cornell University opened in 1865, and
   today it is known as _____ excellent university — one of the best universities in the world.

PRACTICE 7 ▸ Count and noncount nouns. (Charts 11-2 → 11-4)
Which of the words can follow **one** and which can follow **some**? Write the correct form for each noun.
If the noun does not have a singular form, write **Ø**.

	one	**some**
1. word	*word*	*words*
2. vocabulary	*Ø*	*vocabulary*
3. slang		
4. homework		
5. assignment		
6. dress		
7. clothing		
8. family		
9. knowledge		
10. information		
11. fact		
12. luck		
13. cup		
14. coffee		
15. question		

---

philanthropist = a rich person who gives a lot of money to help poor people or good causes.

PRACTICE 8 ▶ Count and noncount nouns. (Charts 11-2 → 11-5)

Complete the sentences with the correct words from the box. Use the plural
form as necessary.

apple tree	corn	jewel	machine	pea	scenery
bracelet	equipment	jewelry	machinery	rice	tool
✓ bread	grass	lake	mountain	ring	

1. I went to the grocery store and bought some _______*bread,*_______

____

2. I stood on a hill in the countryside and saw some _______________

____

3. At the auto repair shop, I saw some _______________________

____

4. I went to a jewelry store and saw some _______________________

____

PRACTICE 9 ▶ Count and noncount nouns. (Charts 11-2 → 11-5)

Complete the sentences with **one**, **much**, or **many**.
Do you have …

1. _____*one*_____ chair?
2. _____*much*_____ furniture?
3. _____*many*_____ vegetables?
4. _____________ fruit?
5. _____________ water?
6. _____________ sand?
7. _____________ clothing?
8. _____________ clothes?
9. _____________ child?
10. _____________ money?
11. _____________ facts?
12. _____________ information?
13. _____________ stuff?
14. _____________ thing?
15. _____________ things?
16. _____________ problems?

PRACTICE 10 ▶ *Many* vs. *much*. (Chart 11-5)

Complete the sentences with the correct words in *italics*. Use the plural form of the noun
where necessary.

1. *apple, coffee, fruit, sugar, vegetable*

   a. I didn't buy many _____*apples*_____ or _______________.

   b. I didn't buy much _____*coffee*_____, _______________, or _______________.

2. *English, answer, person, slang, thing*

   a. Mr. Wade doesn't know many _______________, _______________ and _______________.

   b. Mr. Wade doesn't know much _______________ or _______________.

3. *homework, idea, information, suggestion, work*

   a. Does Sue have many _______________ or _______________?

   b. Does Sue have much _______________, _______________ or _______________?

4. *crime, garbage, police officer, traffic, violence*

    a. Does this city have many _________________?

    b. Does this city have much _________, _________, _________, or _________?

PRACTICE 11 ▸ *How many* and *how much*. (Chart 11-5)

Complete the questions with **many** or **much**. Add final **-s/-es** if necessary to make a noun plural. (Some of the count nouns have irregular plural forms.) If a verb is needed, circle the correct one. If final **-s/-es** is not necessary, write **Ø**.

1. How _______*many*_______ **letter** ___*s*___ is / (are) there in the English alphabet?*

2. How _______*much*_______ **mail** __*Ø*__ did you get yesterday?

3. How _______*many*_______ **man** __*men*__ has / (have) a full beard at least once in their life?

4. How _______________ English **literature** _______ have you studied?

5. How _______________ English **word** _______ do you know?

6. How _______________ **gasoline** _______ does it take to fill the tank in your car?

7. (*British:* How _______________ **petrol** _______ does it take to fill the tank?)

8. How _______________ **grandchild** _______ does Mrs. Cunningham have?

9. How _______________ **fun** _______ did you have at the amusement park?

10. How _______________ **island** _______ is / are there in Indonesia?**

11. How _______________ **people** _______ will there be by the year 2050?***

12. How _______________ **zero** _______ is / are there in a billion?****

PRACTICE 12 ▸ Review: count and noncount nouns. (Charts 11-1 → 11-5)

Choose all the words that can be used with each given noun.

1. flower	(a)	an	some	much	many
2. flowers	a	an	(some)	much	(many)
3. coin	a	an	some	much	many
4. money	a	an	some	much	many
5. coins	a	an	some	much	many
6. salt	a	an	some	much	many
7. error	a	an	some	much	many
8. mistake	a	an	some	much	many
9. honest mistake	a	an	some	much	many
10. mistakes	a	an	some	much	many
11. dream	a	an	some	much	many
12. interesting dream	a	an	some	much	many
13. questions	a	an	some	much	many

---

* There are twenty-six (26) letters in the English alphabet.

** More than thirteen thousand seven hundred (13,700).

*** Estimated at nearly ten billion (10,000,000,000).

**** Nine (9)

14.	soap	a	an	some	much	many
15.	bar of soap	a	an	some	much	many
16.	beauty	a	an	some	much	many
17.	cup of tea	a	an	some	much	many
18.	unsafe place	a	an	some	much	many
19.	fruit	a	an	some	much	many
20.	pieces of fruit	a	an	some	much	many

PRACTICE 13 ▸ *A few* vs. *a little*. (Chart 11-5)

Complete the sentences with ***a few*** or ***a little***. Add a final ***-s/-es/-ies*** to the noun if necessary. Otherwise, write **Ø**.

1. Everyone needs ______ *a little* ______ **help** __Ø__ sometimes.

2. The children's native language is Spanish, but they speak ________________ **English** ______ .

3. We bought ________________ **orange** ______ to make fresh orange juice.

4. I like ________________ **sugar** ______ in my coffee.

5. I'm going to give you ________________ **advice** ______ .

6. I need ________________ **suggestion** ______ .

7. He asked ________________ **question** ______ .

8. We talked to ________________ **people** ______ on the plane.

9. Please give me ________________ more **minute** ______ .

10. I have ________________ **work** ______ to do over the weekend.

11. Pedro already knew ________________ English **grammar** ______ before he took this English course.

12. I've been making ________________ **progress** ______ in the last couple of weeks.

PRACTICE 14 ▸ Count and noncount nouns: summary. (Chart 11-5)

Choose all the expressions of quantity that can be used to complete the sentences.

1. My teacher assigned _____ vocabulary for review.

   a. a lot of

   b. some

   c. a little

   d. a few

   e. too much

   f. too many

   g. several

   h. twenty

2. My teacher assigned _____ words for review.

   a. a lot of

   b. some

   c. a little

   d. a few

   e. too much

   f. too many

   g. several

   h. twenty

3. I ate _____ fruit.

  a. some

  b. a little

  c. a few

  d. too many

  e. too much

4. I ate _____ apples.

  a. several

  b. many

  c. too much

  d. some

  e. a lot of

5. There is _____ traffic in the street.

  a. several

  b. some

  c. too many

  d. a little

  e. a lot of

  f. a few

  g. too much

  h. five

6. There are _____ cars in the street.

  a. several

  b. some

  c. too many

  d. a little

  e. a lot of

  f. a few

  g. too much

  h. five

PRACTICE 15 ▸ Count and noncount nouns. (Charts 11-1 → 11-5)

Add *-s* where necessary.

Plants

(1) Scientist _____ divide living things into two groups: animal _____ and plant _____. Animals move around from one place _____ to another, but plants don't. Plants stay in one place.

(2) Many plants, such as flower _____, grass, and tree _____, grow on land. Some plants grow only in desert _____, and some grow only in ocean _____. There are a few plants that grow on the tops of mountain _____ and even in the polar regions.

(3) Plants that people grow for food are called crops. Rice _____ is a crop _____ that grows in many parts of the world _____. Other common crops include potatoes, wheat, and corn. All crop _____ depend on nature. Bad weather _____, such as too much or too little rain, can destroy wheat or corn field _____.

(4) Plant _____ are also important to our health _____. We get a lot of medicines from plants. In addition, plants clean the air _____. Many tree _____ and other plants remove bad gasses from the atmosphere and release oxygen into the air. The more plants we have on earth _____, the healthier the air _____ is.

Choose the correct answers.

1. We have been to Italy several _______.	a. chicken
2. My grandparents have a small farm with about 50 _______.	b. chickens
3. On the table there were plates, forks, knives, and _______.	c. hair
4. Drivers should turn on their _______ before it gets dark.	d. hairs
5. Please open the curtains. There's not enough _______ in this room.	e. time
6. Rosa is 40. She has a few gray _______.	f. times
7. A fish bowl is made of _______.	g. glass
8. I don't like beef, but I do like _______.	h. glasses
9. Al is getting bald. He is losing his _______.	i. light
10. I couldn't finish the exam. There wasn't enough _______.	j. lights

PRACTICE 17 ▸ Units of measure with noncount nouns. (Chart 11-7)

What units of measure are usually used with the following nouns? More than one unit of measure can be used with some of the nouns.

bag   bottle   box   can   jar

1. a _______*jar*_______ of pickles
2. a _______________ of aspirin
3. a _______________ of cereal
4. a _______________ of honey
5. a _______________ of sardines

6. a _______________ of sugar
7. a _______________ of peanut butter
8. a _______________ of soy sauce
9. a _______________ of uncooked noodles
10. a _______________ of beans

PRACTICE 18 ▸ Units of measure with noncount nouns. (Chart 11-7)

Complete the sentences with the correct words from the box. Use the plural form if necessary. Some sentences have more than one possible completion.

bottle	cup	glass	loaf	pound
carton	gallon	kilo	piece	sheet

1. I drank a _______*cup*_______ of coffee.
2. I bought two _______*pounds/kilos*_______ of flour.
3. I drank a _______________ of orange juice.
4. I put ten _______________ of gas in my car.
5. I bought a _______________ of milk at the supermarket.
6. I need a _______________ of eggs.
7. I used two _______________ of bread to make a sandwich.
8. There is a _______________ of fruit on the table.
9. There are 200 _______________ of lined paper in my notebook.
10. I bought one _______________ of bread at the store.

11. Let me give you a _________________ of advice.

12. I just learned an interesting _________________ of information.

PRACTICE 19 ▶ *Much* vs. *many*. (Charts 11-5 → 11-7)

Complete the questions with **much** or **many** and the appropriate noun.

Going on a Trip

1. A: Are you all packed for your trip to Tahiti? How ____*many suitcases*____ are you taking with you?

   B: Three. (I'm taking three suitcases.)

2. A: How ____*much sunscreen*____ are you taking?

   B: A lot. (I'm taking a lot of sunscreen.)

3. A: How _________________ are you taking?

   B: Two pairs. (I'm taking two pairs of sandals.)

4. A: How _________________ did you pack?

   B: One tube. (I packed one tube of toothpaste.)

5. A: How _________________ will you and Sandy have?

   B: I'm not sure. Maybe 20 kilos. (We may have 20 kilos of luggage.)

6. A: How _________________ will you pay in overweight baggage charges?

   B: A lot. (We will pay of lot of money for overweight baggage.)

7. A: How _________________ will you be away?

   B: Twelve. (We'll be away for twelve days.)

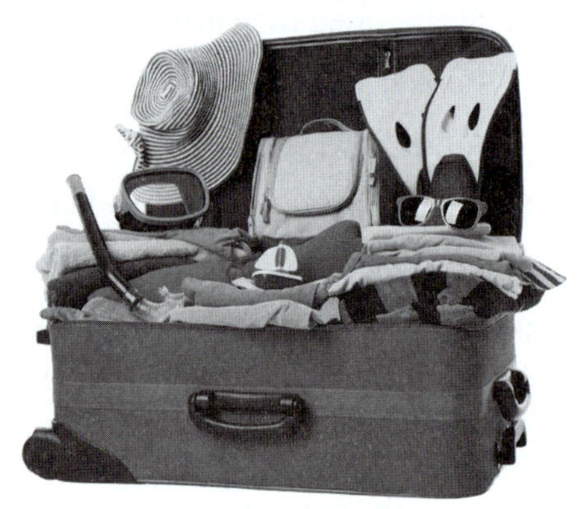

PRACTICE 20 ▶ Specific vs. non-specific nouns. (Chart 11-8)

Decide if the words in green have a specific or non-specific meaning.

1. The *movie* that we watched last night was excellent.   (specific)   non-specific

2. How often do you watch *movies*?   specific   non-specific

3. There are a lot of good *restaurants* in this city.   specific   non-specific

4. The *food* at this restaurant is amazing.   specific   non-specific

5. The *dishes* in the sink are dirty.   specific   non-specific

6. I don't like washing *dishes*.   specific   non-specific

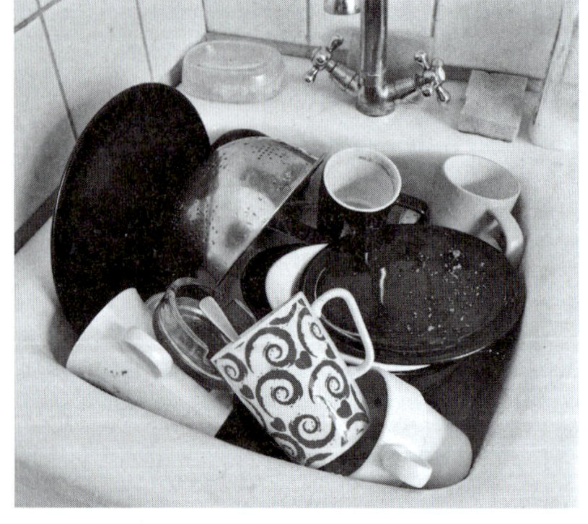

PRACTICE 21 ▶ *A/an* vs. *some*. (Charts 11-5 and 11-8)

Complete the sentences with ***a/an, the,*** or ***Ø.***

1. A: Could you please put   a / the / Ø   milk back in   a / the / Ø   fridge?

   B: Sorry! I forgot to put it back earlier.

   A: Don't worry about it, but let's straighten up   a / the / Ø   kitchen. I'll sweep   a / the / Ø
   floor. Could you please take out   a / the / Ø   trash and clean   a / the / Ø   counters?

   B: Yes, of course.

2. A: We need to work on   a / the / Ø   our homework project today. Why don't we meet in front
   of   a / the / Ø   library at 4:00?

   B: I'll be at   a / the / Ø   work then. Can we meet tomorrow instead?

   A: Sure. What's   a / the / Ø   best time for you tomorrow?

   B: I'm free all day, but I would prefer to meet in   a / the / Ø   morning.

3. A: Why weren't you in   a / the / Ø   class yesterday?

   B: I had to stay   a / the / Ø   home to take care of   a / the / Ø
   my daughter.

   A: Why wasn't she at   a / the / Ø   school?

   B: She fell and hurt   a / the / Ø   her arm.

   A: Oh no! Did she get   an / the / Ø   X-ray?

   B: Yes, and   a / the / Ø   X-ray results were not good. She broke
   a bone. She has to wear   a / the / Ø   cast for two months.
   A / The / Ø   cast is really uncomfortable.

   A: I'm sorry to hear   a / the / Ø   this terrible news! Is this
   a / the / Ø   first time that she has broken a bone?

   B: Yes, it is. Let's hope it is also   a / the / Ø   last!

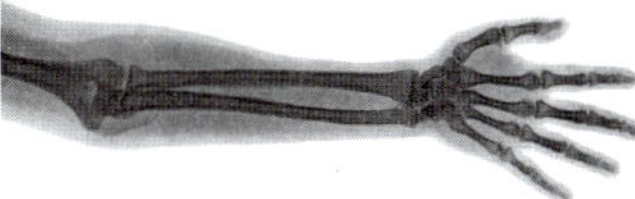

an x-ray

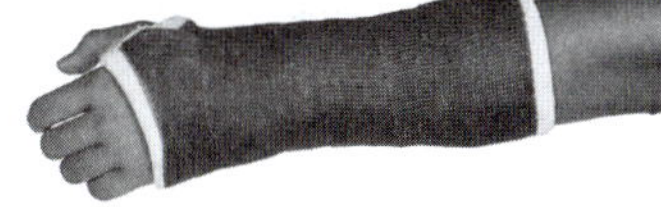

a cast

PRACTICE 22 ▶ *A/an* vs. *the*: singular count nouns. (Charts 11-8 and 11-9)

Complete the sentences with ***a/an*** or ***the***.

1. A: _____*A*_____ dog makes a good pet.

   B: I agree.

2. A: Did you feed _____*the*_____ dog?

   B: Yes, I did.

3. My dorm room has _________ desk, _________ bed, _________ chest of drawers, and two chairs.

4. A: Jessica, where's the stapler?

   B: On _________ desk. If it's not there, look in _________ top drawer.

5. A: Sara, put your bike in _________ garage before dark.

   B: Okay, Dad.

6. Our house has _________ garage. We keep our car and our bikes there.

7. Almost every sentence has _________ subject and _________ verb.

8. Look at this sentence: *Luca lives in Miami.* What is _________ subject, and what is _________ verb?

9. A: What time does __________ meeting start Tuesday?

   B: 8:00.

10. A: I can't see you at 4:00. I'll be in __________ meeting then. How about 4:30?

    B: Fine.

11. Max's car ran out of gas. He didn't have cell phone reception, so he had to walk __________ long

    distance to find __________ telephone and call his brother for help.

12. __________ distance from __________ sun to __________ earth is 93,000,000 miles.

13. A: Where do you live?

    B: We live on __________ quiet street in the suburbs.

14. A: Is this __________ street where Jamie lives?

    B: Yes, it is.

PRACTICE 23 ▸ Using *the* for second mention. (Chart 11-9)

Complete the sentences with **a/an**, **some**, or **the**. Note: Use **the** when a noun is mentioned for the second time.

1. I had __________ soup and __________ sandwich for lunch. __________ soup was too salty, but

   __________ sandwich was pretty good.

2. Yesterday I bought __________ clothes. I bought __________ suit, __________ shirt, and __________ tie.

   __________ suit is gray and comes with a vest. __________ shirt is pale blue, and __________ tie has

   black and gray stripes.

3. A: I saw __________ accident yesterday.

   B: Oh? Where?

   A: On Grand Avenue. __________ man in __________ Volkswagen drove through a stop sign and hit

      __________ bus.

   B: Was anyone hurt in __________ accident?

   A: I don't think so. __________ man who was driving __________ Volkswagen got out of his car and

      seemed to be okay. His car was only slightly damaged. No one on __________ bus was hurt.

4. Yesterday I saw __________ man and __________ woman. They were having __________ argument.

   __________ man was yelling at __________ woman, and __________ woman was shouting at __________

   man. I don't know what __________ argument was about.

5. I read __________ interesting book. __________ book last month. __________ book was about

   __________ woman who hiked a very long trail in California. __________ trail was over 1,000 miles

   long. __________ woman didn't have any hiking experience, but she was able to complete __________

   trail in 94 days.

Complete the sentences with **a/an**, **some**, or **the**.

One day last month while I was driving through the countryside, I saw ____*a*____ man and
1

__________ truck next to __________ covered bridge. __________ bridge crossed __________ small river.
2   3   4   5

I stopped and asked __________ man, "What's the matter? Can I help?"
6

"Well," said __________ man, "My truck is about a half-inch* too tall. Or maybe __________ top of
7   8

__________ bridge is a half-inch too short. Either way, my truck won't fit under __________ bridge."
9   10

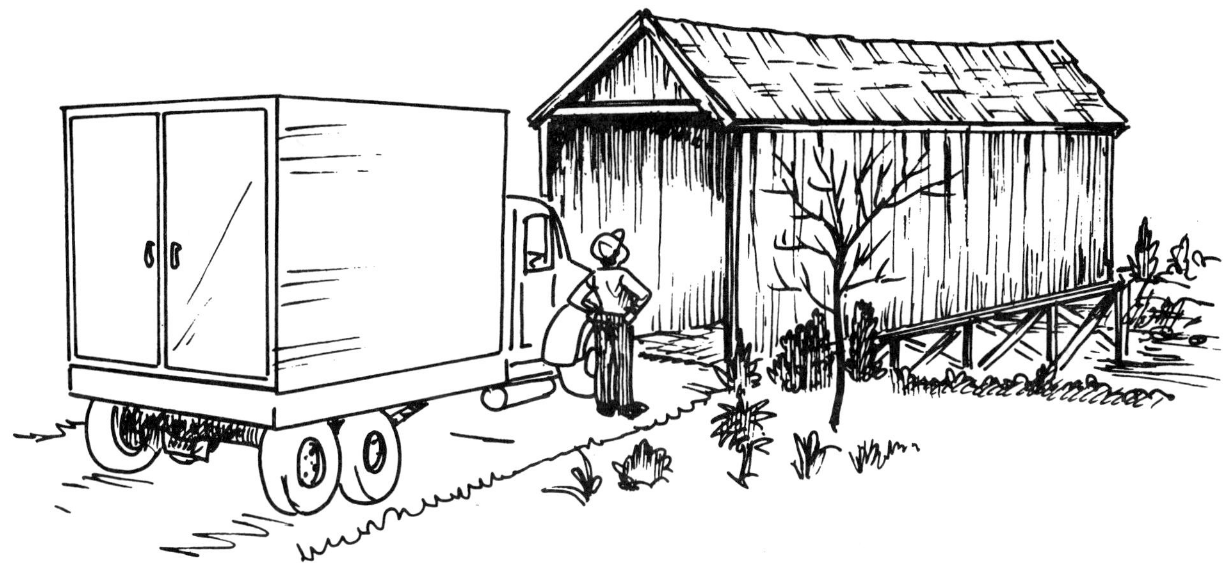

"Hmmm. There must be __________ solution to this problem," I said.
11

"I don't know. I guess I'll have to turn around and take another route," he replied.

After a few moments of thought, I said, "I have __________ solution!"
12

"What is it?" asked the man.

"Let a little air out of your tires. Then __________ truck won't be too tall, and you can cross
13

__________ bridge over __________ river."
14   15

"Hey, that's __________ great idea. Let's try it!" So __________ man let a little air out of __________
16   17   18

tires and was able to cross __________ river and go on his way.
19

---

*One-half inch = 1.27 centimeters

PRACTICE 25 ▸ Summary: *a/an* vs. *the* vs. Ø. (Chart 11-8 and 11-9)
Complete the sentences with ***a/an, the***, or **Ø**. Add capital letters as necessary.

1. It is __________ fact: __________ steam rises when __________ water boils.

2. __________ gas is expensive nowadays.

3. __________ gas I got yesterday cost more than I've ever paid.

4. __________ sun is __________ star. We need __________ sun for __________ heat, __________ light, and
   __________ energy.

5. A: Do you see __________ man who is standing next to Janet?

   B: Yes. Who is he?

   A: He's __________ president of this university.

6. A: How is __________ your sister? __________ last time I saw her, she was working at __________
   coffee shop. Does she still work at __________ same place?

   B: No. That was a very long time ago! Now she is __________ attorney. She works at __________ law
   firm in Chicago.

7. __________ pizza originated in Italy. It is a pie with __________ cheese, __________ tomatoes, and
   other things on top.

8. A: Hey, Nick. Pass __________ pizza. I want another piece.

   B: There are only two pieces left. You take __________ big piece, and I'll take __________ small one.

9. I had __________ interesting experience yesterday. __________ man in __________ blue suit came into
   my office and handed me __________ bouquet of __________ flowers. I had never seen __________ man
   before in my life, but I thanked him for __________ flowers. Then he walked out __________ door.

PRACTICE 26 ▸ Using *the* or Ø with names. (Chart 11-10)
Complete the sentences with ***the*** or **Ø**.

1. Ingrid has been in Orly Airport several times, but she has never visited ____Ø____ Paris.

2. ____Ø____ Dr. James was the youngest person at her university to get a Ph.D.

3. __________ Mount Rainier in Washington is in __________ Cascade Mountain Range.

4. __________ Nile is the longest river in __________ Africa.

5. Is __________ Toronto or __________ Montreal the largest city in Canada?

6. During her tour of Africa, Helen climbed __________ Mount Kilimanjaro and visited several national
   parks in __________ Kenya.

7. __________ New Zealand is made up of two islands: North Island and South Island.

8. __________ Himalayas extend through several countries, including Pakistan, __________ India, and
   __________ Nepal.

9. __________ President Davis was surprised to be elected to a fourth term.

10. __________ Ho Chi Minh City in __________ Vietnam was formerly called __________ Saigon.

11. __________ Andes Mountains in South America extend for 5000 miles.

12. __________ Dominican Republic and __________ Haiti share an island called Hispaniola. __________
    Atlantic Ocean is at the north, and __________ Caribbean Sea is at the south.

Answer the questions. Choose from the list below. Use ***the*** if necessary. (Not all names on the list will be used.)

Africa	Europe	Mont Blanc	Saudi Arabia
Alps	Gobi Desert	Mount Vesuvius	Shanghai
Amazon River	Indian Ocean	Nepal	South America
Beijing	Lagos	Netherlands	Taipei
Black Sea	Lake Baikal	Nile River	Thames River
✓ Dead Sea	Lake Tanganyika	North America	United Arab Emirates
Elbe River	Lake Titicaca	Sahara Desert	Urals

Geography Trivia

Question   **Answer**

1. What is the lowest point on earth?   *the Dead Sea*

2. What is the second-longest river in the world?   _______________

3. What is the most populated city in China?   _______________

4. What is the largest desert in the world?   _______________

5. What river runs through London?   _______________

6. On what continent is the Volga River?   _______________

7. What mountains border France and Italy?   _______________

8. What lake is in east central Africa?   _______________

9. On what continent is Mexico?   _______________

10. What is the third-largest ocean in the world?   _______________

11. What country is also known as Holland?   _______________

12. What is the third-largest continent in the world? _______________

13. What country is located in the Himalayas?   _______________

14. What mountains are part of the boundary between
    Europe and Asia?   _______________

15. What is the capital of Nigeria?   _______________

16. What country consists of seven kingdoms?   _______________

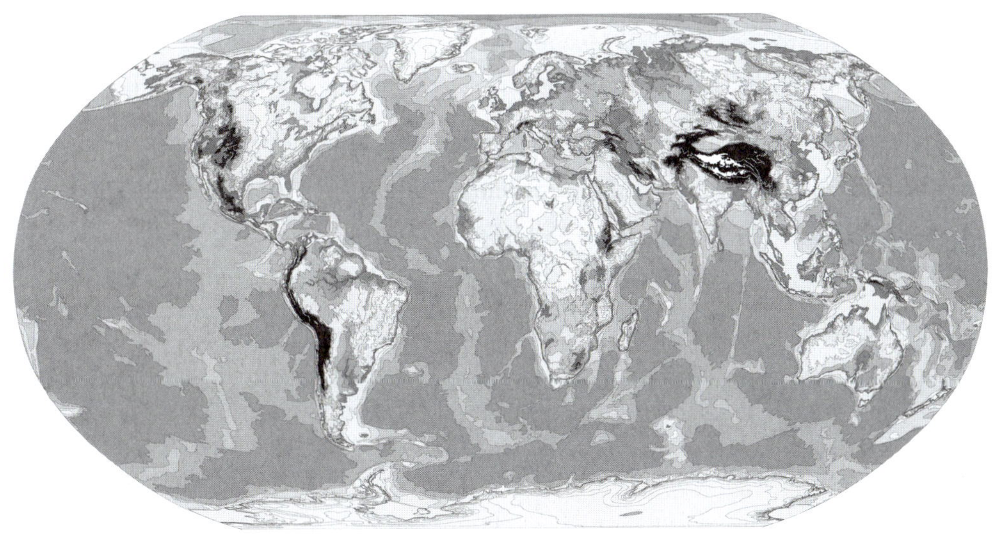

PRACTICE 28 ▶ Capitalization. (Chart 11-11)
Add capital letters where necessary.

              B

1. I'm taking ~~b~~iology 101 this semester.
2. I'm taking history, biology, english, and calculus this semester.
3. Some lab classes meet on saturday.
4. My roommate likes vietnamese food, and i like thai food.
5. Shelia works for the xerox corporation. it is a very large corporation.
6. Pedro is from latin america. He speaks spanish.
7. My favorite park is central park in new york.
8. Do you know my uncle?
9. I like uncle joe and aunt sara.
10. susan w. miller is a professor.
11. I am in prof. miller's class.
12. In january, it's winter in canada and summer in argentina.
13. I would like to visit los angeles.
14. It's the largest city in california.

PRACTICE 29 ▶ Check your knowledge. (Chapter 11 Review)
Correct the errors.

                                 letter

1. The mail carrier brought only one ~~mail~~ today.
2. Mr. Dale gave his class long history assignment for the weekend.
3. Tariq speaks several language, including Arabic and German.
4. I usually have glass water with my lunch.
5. A helpful police officer gave us an information about the city.
6. This recipe calls for two cup of nut.
7. Much vegetable are believed to have cancer-fighting ingredients.
8. Only applicants with the necessary experiences should apply for the position.
9. When Vicki likes a movie, she sees it several time.
10. A popular children's stories is *Snow White and the Seven Dwarfs*.
11. Is it possible to stop all violences in the world?
12. Some of the homeworks for my English class was easy, but many of the assignment were unclear.
13. Diane has been to Hong Kong several time recently. She always has wonderful time.
14. Many parents need advices about raising children.
15. A person doesn't need many equipment to play baseball: just ball and a bat.
16. I usually go to school in morning, and I work in afternoon.
17. I need to buy some furnitures for my new apartment.
18. The beaches in my country have the beautiful sands.

Complete the puzzle. Use the clues to find the correct words. All the words are from Chapter 11.

Across

1. There isn't much _______________ from the earthquake area. All the communication lines are down, and we can't get any news.

8. Our teacher gave us some good _______________ to find helpful websites.

9. Please hurry. We don't have much _______________.

10. There are too _______________ cars on the road.

Down

2. I wanted to buy some candy, so my grandfather gave me a _______________ dollars.

3. The doctor gave me some good _______________: Exercise regularly.

4. I have seen this movie four _______________.

5. My grandmother handed me a _______________ money — about 10 dollars.

6. You don't need _______________ equipment to play tennis: just a tennis racket and some tennis balls.

7. I was afraid to hear the truth, but now I am glad you told me everything. I appreciate your

_______________.

Adjective Clauses

PRACTICE 1 ▸ Adjective clauses: introduction. (Chart 12-1)

Check (✓) the items that have complete sentences.

1. __✓__ I have a friend.

2. __✓__ She lives in New Zealand.

3. _____ I have a friend lives in New Zealand.

4. _____ Who lives in New Zealand.

5. __✓__ Who lives in New Zealand?

6. __✓__ I have a friend who lives in New Zealand.

7. __✓__ My friend lives in New Zealand.

8. _____ My friend who lives in New Zealand.

PRACTICE 2 ▸ Using *who* and *that* in adjective clauses to describe people. (Charts 12-2)

<u>Underline</u> the adjective clause in the first sentence. Then change the sentence into two simple sentences.*

1. *Complex sentence:* I thanked the man <u>who helped me move the refrigerator</u>.

   Simple sentence 1: ______*I thanked*______ the man.

   Simple sentence 2: ______*He helped*______ me move the refrigerator.

2. *Complex sentence:* A woman who was wearing a gray suit asked me for directions.

   Simple sentence 1: ___A woman asked___ me for directions.

   Simple sentence 2: ___She was wearing___ a gray suit.

3. *Complex sentence:* I saw a man that was wearing a blue coat.

   Simple sentence 1: ___I saw___ a man.

   Simple sentence 2: ___He was wearing___ a blue coat.

4. *Complex sentence:* The girl that broke the vase apologized to Mrs. Cook.

   Simple sentence 1: ___The girl apologized___ to Mrs. Cook.

   Simple sentence 2: ___She broke___ the vase.

---

*A simple sentence has only an independent clause. For example:

    I thanked the man. = a simple sentence consisting of one independent clause

    He helped me. = a simple sentence consisting of one independent clause

*A complex sentence has an independent clause and one or more dependent clauses. For example:

    I thanked the man who helped me. = a complex sentence consisting of one independent clause (*I thanked the man*) and one dependent clause (*who helped me*)

5. *Complex sentence:* The parents hugged the boy who had pulled his
brother from the icy river.

Simple sentence 1: <u>The parents hugged</u> the boy.

Simple sentence 2: <u>He had pulled</u> his brother
from the icy river.

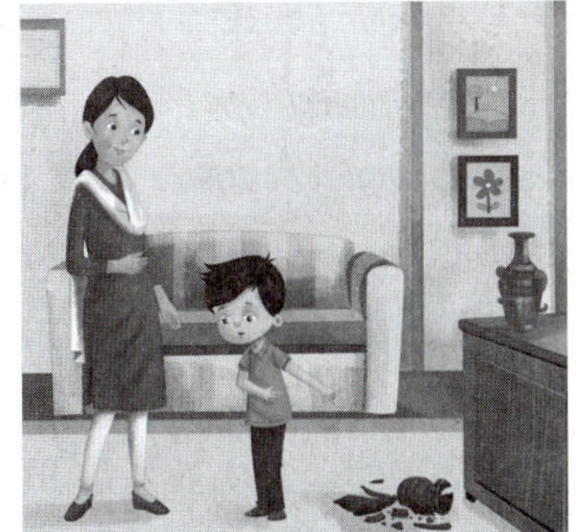

PRACTICE 3 ▸ Using *who* and *that* in adjective clauses to describe people. (Chart 12-2)

<u>Underline</u> each adjective clause. Then write "S" above its subject and "V" above its verb.

1. The people <u>who live next to me</u> are nice.
2. My neighbors who live across the street have a new baby.
3. A family that is from India just moved next door.
4. Our neighborhood is a good place for people who have children.
5. A professor who teaches at the university just moved to our street.
6. One of my neighbors has a disabled child who is training to play basketball in the Special Olympics.

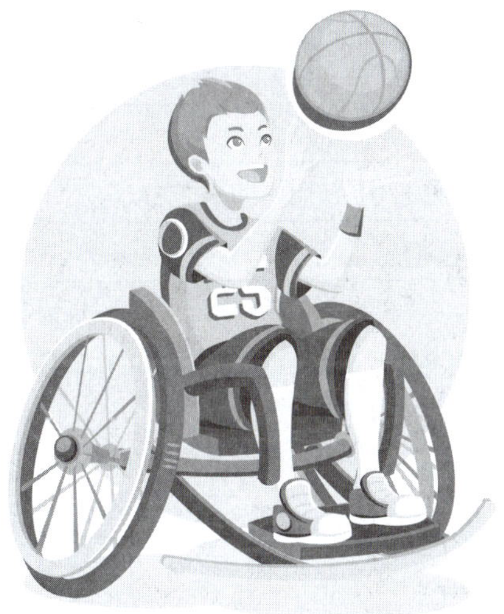

PRACTICE 4 ▸ Using *who* and *that* in adjective clauses to describe people. (Chart 12-2)

Combine the two short sentences into one long sentence using "short sentence 2" as an adjective clause.
Write two sentences: the first with ***who*** and the second with ***that***.

1. *Simple sentence 1:* The woman was polite.

   Simple sentence 2: She answered the phone.

   Complex sentence 1: The woman <u>who answered the phone</u> was polite.

   Complex sentence 2: The woman <u>that answered the phone</u> was polite.

2. *Simple sentence 1:* The man is also a singer.

   Simple sentence 2: The man played the guitar.

   Complex sentence 1: The man _______________________________________ is also a singer.

   Complex sentence 2: The man _______________________________________ is also a singer.

3. *Simple sentence 1:*   I read about the soccer player.

   Simple sentence 2:   He was injured yesterday.

   Complex sentence 1:   I read about the soccer player ________________________ yesterday.

   Complex sentence 2:   I read about the soccer player ________________________ yesterday.

4. *Simple sentence 1:*   I know a man.

   Simple sentence 2:   He has sailed around the world.

   Complex sentence 1:   I know a man
   ________________________ around the world.

   Complex sentence 2:   I know a man
   ________________________ around the world.

PRACTICE 5 ▶ Using *who* and *that* in adjective clauses to describe people. (Chart 12-2)

Complete the sentences using either **who** or **that**.

1. A hair cutter is a person ______ *who / that cuts hair* ______.

2. A pizza maker is a person ________________________.

3. A tennis player is a person ________________________.

4. An English teacher is a person ________________________.

5. A horse trainer is a person ________________________.

6. A meat eater is a person ________________________.

7. Tea drinkers are people ________________________.

8. Firefighters are people ________________________.

PRACTICE 6 ▶ Using object pronouns in adjective clauses to describe people. (Chart 12-3)

Combine each pair of sentences using an adjective clause.

1. The woman was polite. Jack met her.

   *Use **that**:*   The woman ______ *that Jack met* ______ was polite.

2. The woman was very tall. Jack saw her.

   *Use **Ø**:*   The woman ________________________ was very tall.

3. The woman is a professor. Jack knows her.

   *Use **that**:*   The woman ________________________ is a professor.

4. The student was grateful. The teacher helped the student.

   *Use **that**:*   The student ________________________ was grateful.

5. The student was happy about the exam. I helped the student.

   *Use **Ø**:*   The student ________________________ was happy about the exam.

6. The student won a scholarship. I just met the student.

   *Use **who**:*   The student ________________________ won a scholarship.

7. The student is the class president. You see the student over there.

   *Use **whom**:*   The student ________________________ is the class president.

PRACTICE 7 ▸ Using *who* and *that* in adjective clauses. (Charts 12-2 and 12-3)

Write "S" if *who* or *that* is the subject of the adjective clause. Write "O" if *who* or *that* is the object of the adjective clause. Cross out the words *who* or *that* where possible.

1. __S__ The students **who** go to this school are friendly.

2. __O__ The people ~~that~~ I saw in the park were practicing yoga.

3. _____ I saw several people **who** were practicing yoga.

4. _____ I know the woman **that** my uncle hired.

5. _____ I like the woman **who** manages my uncle's store.

6. _____ Do you like the mechanic **that** fixed your car?

7. _____ Mr. Polanski is a mechanic **that** you can trust.

8. _____ What's the name of the woman **that** Hank invited to the dance?

9. _____ Do you know the man **who**'s dancing with Katrina?

10. _____ The singer **that** we just heard comes from Mexico.

11. _____ The singer **who** just performed comes from Mexico.

PRACTICE 8 ▸ Using object pronouns in adjective clauses to describe people. (Chart 12-3)

Choose <u>all</u> the correct answers.

1. A man _____ works on a submarine.
   a. I know
   b. whom I know
   c. who I know
   d. that I know

2. I know a man _____ on a submarine.
   a. works
   b. he works
   c. who works
   d. that works

3. My mother is a woman _____ tremendously.
   a. I admire
   b. whom I admire
   c. who I admire
   d. that I admire

4. My mother is a woman _____.
   a. is always optimistic
   b. she is always optimistic
   c. who is always optimistic
   d. that is always optimistic

5. I'm pleased with the person _____.
   a. he is going to be our next mayor
   b. who is going to be our next mayor
   c. whom is going to be our next mayor
   d. that is going to be our next mayor

6. I'm pleased with the person _____.
   a. the people elected
   b. that the people elected
   c. who the people elected
   d. the people elected him.

In the box, write every possible pronoun that can be used to connect the adjective clause to the main clause: **who**, **that**, or **whom**. Also, write Ø if the pronoun can be omitted.

1. The woman [who / that] sat next to me on the plane was very friendly.

2. The woman [that / Ø / who / whom] I met on the plane was very friendly.

3. Two people [ ] I didn't know walked into the classroom.

4. The people [ ] walked into the classroom were strangers.

5. My cousin's wife is the woman [ ] is talking to Mr. Horn.

6. I like the woman [ ] my brother and I met on the bus.

PRACTICE 10 ▶ *Who* vs. *that*. (Charts 12-2 → 12-4)

Choose <u>all</u> the correct answers.

1. The magazine _____ I read on the plane was interesting.

   a. who   (b.) that

2. The artist _____ drew my picture is very good.

   (a.) who   (b.) that

3. I really enjoyed the experiences _____ I had on my trip to Nigeria.

   a. who   b. that

4. Most of the games _____ we played as children no longer entertain us.

   a. who   b. that

5. All the people _____ I called yesterday can come to the meeting on Monday.

   a. who   b. that

6. The teacher _____ was ill canceled her math class.

   a. who   b. that

7. The flight _____ I took to Singapore was on time.

   a. who   b. that

8. I read an article _____ discussed the current political crisis.

   a. who   b. that

Write "S" if *that* is the subject of the adjective clause. Write "O" if *that* is the object of the adjective clause. Cross out the word *that* where possible.

1. __O__ The medicine ~~that~~ the doctor prescribed for me was very expensive.

2. __S__ The medicine **that** is on the shelf is no longer good.

3. _____ The computer **that** I bought recently has already crashed several times.

4. _____ The car **that** my husband drives is very reliable.

5. _____ The house **that** sits on top of the hill has won several architecture awards.

6. _____ The restaurant **that** offered low-cost dinners to senior citizens has recently closed.

7. _____ The trees **that** shade our house are over 300 years old.

8. _____ The trees **that** we planted last year have doubled in size.

PRACTICE 12 ▸ Using pronouns in adjective clauses to describe things. (Chart 12-4)

Write the pronouns *which* or *that* that can be used to connect the adjective clause to the main clause. Also write Ø if the pronoun can be omitted.

1. I really enjoyed the movie | *that* / *Ø* / *which* | we saw last night.

2. We saw an exciting movie | | was based on a true story.

3. The plane | | I took to Korea was two hours late because of bad weather.

4. The books | | Jane ordered came in the mail today.

5. Jane was glad to get the books | | came in the mail today.

PRACTICE 13 ▸ Adjective clauses. (Charts 12-3 and 12-4)

Complete the sentences with adjective clauses using the words in *italics*. There is one extra word in each list.

1. *them, I, visited*

   I really miss my relatives ________ *I visited* ________ in Mexico City last year.

2. *I, that, drank, it*

   The coffee ________________ was cold and weak.

3. *wearing, was, I, them*

   The tennis shoes ________________ in the garden got wet and muddy.

4. *that, him, I've, known, and, loved*

   My cousin Ahmed is a person ____ since he was born.

5. *her, I, married, who*

   I have a great deal of respect for the wonderful woman _________________________________
   11 years ago.

6. *have, had, him, we, that*

   The dog _________________________________ for several years is very gentle with young children.

7. *which, it, we, bought*

   The car _________________________________ last year has turned out to be a lemon.*

PRACTICE 14 ▸ Pronouns in adjective clauses. (Charts 12-1 → 12-4)

Choose <u>all</u> the correct answers.

1. I liked the teacher _______ I had for chemistry in high school.

   (a.) who   (b.) whom   (c.) that   d. which   e. Ø

2. I liked chemistry because the teacher _______ taught the class was excellent.

   a. who   b. whom   c. that   d. which   e. Ø

3. The researchers in the Amazon River basin found many plants _______ were previously unknown.

   a. who   b. whom   c. that   d. which   e. Ø

4. The plants _______ the researchers found were carefully taken to a laboratory.

   a. who   b. whom   c. that   d. which   e. Ø

5. Mr. Rice made sandwiches for the children _______ were hungry.

   a. who   b. whom   c. that   d. which   e. Ø

6. The children enjoyed the sandwiches _______ Mr. Rice made for them.

   a. who   b. whom   c. that   d. which   e. Ø

7. Have you read any books by the writer _______ the teacher mentioned in class?

   a. who   b. whom   c. that   d. which   e. Ø

8. A book _______ I read last year has become a best-seller.

   a. who   b. whom   c. that   d. which   e. Ø

9. The fans _______ were sitting in the stadium jumped up and cheered when their team scored a point.

   a. who   b. whom   c. that   d. which   e. Ø

10. The fans jumped up and cheered when their team scored the point _______ won the game.

    a. who   b. whom   c. that   d. which   e. Ø

---

*lemon = something, especially a car, that doesn't work properly and needs a lot of repairs

Choose the correct form of the verb in *italics*. <u>Underline</u> the noun that determines whether the verb in the adjective clause is singular or plural.

1. The <u>students</u> who   is / **are**   in my class come from many countries.

2. The people who   is / are   standing in line to get into the theater have been here for a couple of hours.

3. Water is a chemical compound that   **consists** / consist   of oxygen and hydrogen.

4. There are two students in my class who   speaks / **speak**   Portuguese.

5. I met some people who   knows / **know**   my brother.

6. The student who   **is** / are   talking to the teacher is from Peru.

7. Do you know the people that   lives / **live**   in that house?

8. A carpenter is a person who   makes / make   things out of wood.

9. Sculptors are artists who   **make** / makes   things from clay or other materials.

10. We need to take the bus that   go / **goes**   downtown.

Complete the sentences with adjective clauses. Add prepositions as necessary.

1. We went to a movie. The movie was good.

   a. The movie that ______*we went to*______ was good.

   b. The movie Ø ______*we went to*______ was good.

2. I enjoyed meeting the people yesterday. You introduced me to them.

   a. I enjoyed meeting the people that ____________________________

      yesterday.

   b. I enjoyed meeting the people who ____________________ yesterday.

3. English grammar is a subject. I am quite familiar with English grammar.

   a. English grammar is a subject Ø ____________________.

   b. English grammar is a subject with ____________________.

4. Ms. Perez can help you. You should talk with her.

   a. Ms. Perez is the person Ø ____________________.

   b. Ms. Perez is the person with ____________________.

5. The train is usually late. We are waiting for it.

   a. The train that ____________________ is usually late.

   b. The train Ø ____________________ is usually late.

6. The job requires several years of experience. I'm interested in the job.

   a. The job that ____________________ requires several years of experience.

   b. The job which ____________________ requires several years of experience.

Give all the possible patterns for the adjective clause: *that, which, who, whom,* or *Ø*. Add the necessary prepositions.

1. a. The bus ___*that*___ we were waiting ___*for*___ was an hour late.

   b. The bus ___*which*___ we were waiting ___*for*___ was an hour late.

   c. The bus ___*Ø*___ we were waiting ___*for*___ was an hour late.

   d. The bus for ___*which*___ we were waiting ___*Ø*___ was an hour late.

2. a. The music __________ I listened __________ was pleasant.

   b. The music __________ I listened __________ was pleasant.

   c. The music __________ I listened __________ was pleasant.

   d. The music to __________ I listened __________ was pleasant.

3. a. Psychology is a subject __________ I am very interested __________.

   b. Psychology is a subject __________ I am very interested __________.

   c. Psychology is a subject __________ I am very interested __________.

   d. Psychology is a subject in __________ I am very interested __________.

4. a. The man __________ Maria was arguing __________ was very angry.

   b. The man __________ Maria was arguing __________ was very angry.

   c. The man __________ Maria was arguing __________ was very angry.

   d. The man __________ Maria was arguing__________ was very angry.

   e. The man with __________ Maria was arguing __________ was very angry.

Write the appropriate prepositions or *Ø*. Draw brackets around the adjective clause.

1. I enjoyed the music [we listened ___*to*___ at Sara's apartment.]

2. I paid the shopkeeper for the glass cup [I accidentally broke ___*Ø*___.]

3. The bus we were waiting __________ was only three minutes late.

4. Mrs. Chan is someone I always enjoy talking __________ about politics.

5. I showed my roommate a text message I got from a co-worker __________.

6. One of the subjects I've been interested __________ for a long time is astronomy.

7. The people I talked __________ at the reception were interesting.

8. One of the places I want to visit __________ next year is Mexico City.

9. The website I was looking __________ had useful reviews of local restaurants.

10. The book I wanted __________ wasn't available at the library.

11. English grammar is one of the subjects __________ which I enjoy studying the most.

12. The friend I waved __________ didn't wave back. Maybe he just didn't see me.

13. The woman I introduced you __________ is a famous writer.

14. My brother is someone I usually agree __________, but this time I think he's wrong.

15. The hotel we stayed __________ was really nice.

PRACTICE 19 ▸ Adjective clauses with *whose*. (Chart 12-7)

<u>Underline</u> the adjective clause in each long sentence. Then change the long sentence into two short sentences.

1. *Long sentence:*   I know a man <u>whose daughter is a test-pilot</u>.

   Short sentence 1: ___I know a man___________________.

   Short sentence 2: ___His daughter is a test-pilot_______.

2. *Long sentence:*   The woman whose husband is out of work found a job at JJ's Diner.

   Short sentence 1: ____

   Short sentence 2: ____

3. *Long sentence:*   The man whose wallet I found gave me a reward.

   Short sentence 1: ____

   Short sentence 2: ____

PRACTICE 20 ▸ Adjective clauses with *whose*. (Chart 12-7)

Follow these steps:

1. <u>Underline</u> the possessive word.

2. Draw an arrow to the noun it refers to.

3. Replace the possessive word with ***whose***.

4. Combine the two sentences into one.

1. The firefighters arc vcry brave. <u>Their</u> department has won many awards.

   The firefighters whose department has won many awards are very brave.

2. I talked to the boy. His kite was caught in a tree.

   ____

3. The family is staying in a motel. Their house burned down.

   ____

4. I talked to a woman. Her parents know my parents.

   ____

5. The reporter won an award. Her articles explained genetic engineering.

   ____

6. I know a man. His daughter entered college at the age of 14.

   ____

7. We observed a language teacher. Her teaching methods included role-playing.

   ____

8. The teachers are very popular. Their methods include role-playing.

   ____

PRACTICE 21 ▸ Meaning of adjective clauses. (Charts 12-1 → 12-7)
Check (✓) all the sentences that are true.

1. The policeman who gave Henry a ticket seemed very nervous.

    a. __✓__ Henry received a ticket.

    b. _____ Henry seemed nervous.

    c. __✓__ The policeman seemed nervous.

2. A co-worker of mine whose wife is a pilot is afraid of flying.

    a. _____ My co-worker is a pilot.

    b. _____ My co-worker's wife is afraid of flying.

    c. _____ The pilot is a woman.

3. The man that delivers office supplies to our company bought a Ferrari.

    a. _____ Our company bought a Ferrari.

    b. _____ A man delivers office supplies.

    c. _____ A delivery man bought a Ferrari.

4. The doctor who took care of my father had a heart attack recently.

    a. _____ My father had a heart attack.

    b. _____ The doctor treated a heart attack patient.

    c. _____ The doctor had a heart attack.

5. The forest fire which destroyed two homes in Woodville burned for two weeks.

    a. _____ The forest fire burned for two weeks.

    b. _____ Two homes burned for two weeks.

    c. _____ The forest fire destroyed Woodville.

6. The salesman who sold my friend a used car was arrested for changing the mileage on cars.

    a. _____ My friend bought a car.

    b. _____ My friend was arrested.

    c. _____ The salesman changed the mileage on cars.

PRACTICE 22 ▸ Adjective clauses. (Charts 12-1 → 12-7)
Write all the possible completions: *who, that, which, whose, whom,* or *Ø*.

1. What do you say to people ____*who / that*____ ask you personal questions that you don't want to answer?

2. People _______________ live in New York City are called New Yorkers.

3. Tina likes the present _______________ I gave her for her birthday.

4. George Washington is the president _______________ picture is on a one-dollar bill.

5. Have you seen the movie _______________ won the Best Picture award?

6. Do you know the woman _______________ Michael is engaged to?

7. That's Tom Jenkins. He's the boy _______________ parents live in Switzerland.

8. A thermometer is an instrument _______________ measures temperature.

9. A high-strung person is someone _______________ is always nervous.

10. The man _________________ I told you about is standing over there.

11. In my country, any person _________________ is 18 years old or older can vote. I turned 18 last

    year. The person _________________ I voted for in the national election lost. I hope the

    next candidate for _________________ I vote has better luck.

PRACTICE 23 ▶ Reading. (Chapter 12 Review)
Read the passage. Then choose the correct answers.

Sticky Notes

    Maybe you have a sticky note in this book. Sticky notes are those small, colored papers that
you can stick in books, on your own papers, on walls, and in other places. You may know them as
Post-it® Notes, which was their original name. These notes are common today, but they were not a
product that was planned. Like many other products, the sticky note was invented by accident.

    In 1970, a man named Spencer Silver was working at 3M, a chemical company. The
company was trying to find a strong, new glue that could hold things together. Silver created
a new glue, but the glue was not strong. In fact, it was very weak. The objects he tried to stick
together with the glue soon fell apart. The company didn't use the glue that Silver had created,
but Silver kept it in his desk.

    Four years later, another 3M scientist, Arthur Fry, was singing in a choir. The bookmarks
that he used to mark the songs in his songbook kept falling out. Fry wanted something that
worked better, and he remembered Silver's invention: the glue that was too weak.

    Fry put a small amount of Silver's glue on top of his bookmarks. Success! The bookmarks
on which he had placed the glue stayed on the pages. Even better, they also came off easily
without damaging the pages. Fry and Silver then worked together and developed the glue which
was eventually used on the Post-it® Notes. That glue is on the back of each sticky note.

1. This passage is about ______.
   a. paper that you can stick to something
   b. paper that you use to write letters

2. The sticky notes were a product ______.
   a. that was developed through research
   b. that was the result of an accident

3. Spencer Silver invented a glue ______.
   a. that held things together
   b. that was very weak

4. The company ______.
   a. used Silver's product
   b. didn't find uses for the glue

5. Arthur Fry wanted ______.
   a. bookmarks that stuck to pages
   b. a new book of songs

6. He thought of the invention ______.
   a. that Spencer had made
   b. that 3M was using

7. Fry put some glue ______.
   a. on top of the bookmarks
   b. on top of the book

8. The result was a kind of paper ______.
   a. that stuck very tightly
   b. that stuck, but could also be pulled off easily.

Correct the errors.

looks
1. A movie that ~~look~~ interesting opens tomorrow.

2. My family lived in a house which it was built in 1900.

3. There's the man that we saw him on TV.

4. I don't know people who their lives are carefree.

5. It is important to help people who has no money.

6. At the airport, I was waiting for friends which I hadn't seen them for a long time.

7. The woman live next door likes to relax by doing crossword puzzles every evening.

8. My teacher has two cats who their names are Ping and Pong.

9. I enjoyed the songs which we sang them.

10. The person to that you should speak is Gary Green.

PRACTICE 25 ▸ Word search puzzle. (Chapter 12 Review)

Circle the five words in the puzzle. The words are the pronouns that begin adjective clauses.

The words may be horizontal, vertical, or diagonal. Note: **who** appears as a separate word in addition to appearing inside one of other words.

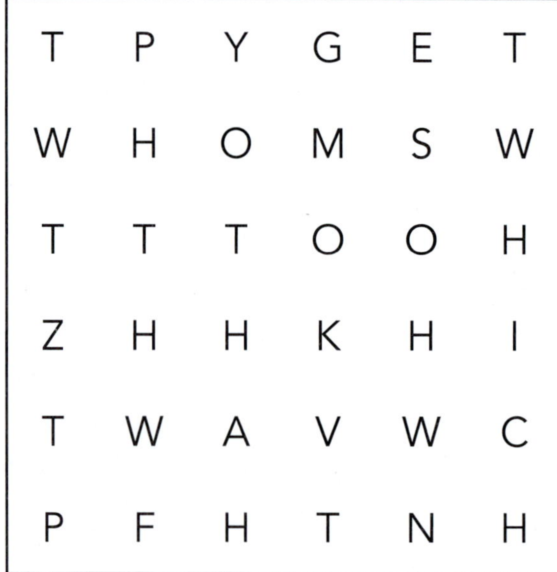

Gerunds and Infinitives

PRACTICE 1 ▶ Verb + gerund. (Chart 13-1)

Complete the sentences with the correct form of the verbs in parentheses.

1. Joan often talks about (*move*) _____*moving*_____ overseas.

2. The Browns sometimes discuss (*live*) _____________ in a smaller town.

3. Christine enjoys (*take*) _____________ care of her young niece.

4. Nathan keeps (*buy*) _____________ lottery tickets, but he never wins.

5. My manager considered (*give*) _____________ pay raises but decided not to.

6. I always put off (*do*) _____________ my math homework.

7. The students finished (*review*) _____________ for the test at 3:00 A.M.

8. Ann talked about (*find*) _____________ a new roommate.

9. Dana quit (*drive*) _____________ after she had a serious car accident.

10. My dentist thinks about (*retire*) _____________, but he enjoys his work too much.

11. Last week, Joan and David postponed (*get married*) _____________ for the second time.

12. Do you mind (*work*) _____________ an extra shift tonight?

PRACTICE 2 ▶ Go + gerund. (Chart 13-2)

Complete each sentence with a form of **go** and a word from the box.

camp	fish	sail	sightsee	skydive
✓dance	hike	shop	ski	swim

1. I love to dance. Last night, my husband and I danced for hours.

   Last night, my husband and I _____*went dancing*_____ .

2. Later this afternoon, Ted is going to take a long walk in the woods.

   Ted _____*will go hiking*_____ later today.

3. Yesterday, Alice visited many stores and bought some clothes and makeup.

   Yesterday, Alice _____*went shopping*_____ .

4. On a hot day, I like to go to the beach and jump in the water.

   On a hot day, I like to _____*go swimming*_____ .

5. My grandfather takes his fishing pole to a pond every Sunday.

   My grandfather _____*goes fishing*_____ every Sunday.

6. When I visit a new city, I like to look around at the sights.

   When I visit a new city, I like to _go sightseeing_ .

7. I love to put up a small tent by a stream, make a fire, and listen to the sounds of the forest during the night.

   I love to _go camping_ .

8. I want to take the sailboat out on the water this afternoon.

   I want to _go sailing_ this afternoon.

9. Once a year, we take our skis to our favorite mountain resort and enjoy an exciting weekend.

   Once a year, we _go skiing_ at our favorite mountain resort.

10. Last year on my birthday, my friends and I went up in an airplane, put on parachutes, and jumped out of the plane at a very high altitude.

    Last year on my birthday, my friends and I _went skydiving_ .

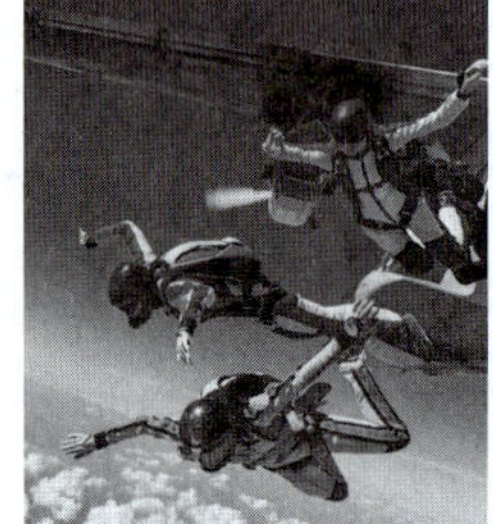 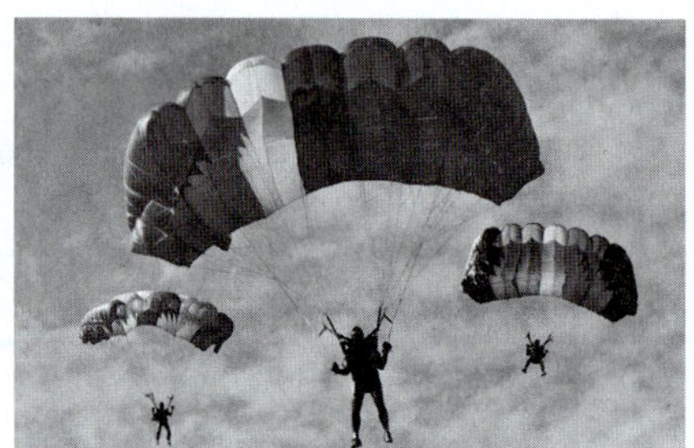

PRACTICE 3 ▸ Identifying gerunds and infinitives. (Charts 13-1 and 13-3)

<u>Underline</u> the gerunds and infinitives in the sentences. Circle "GER" for gerunds and "INF" for infinitives.

1. Ann promised <u>to wait</u> for me.	GER	(INF)
2. I kept <u>walking</u> even though I was tired.	(GER)	INF
3. Alex offered to help me.	GER	INF
4. Karen finished cleaning up the kitchen and went to bed.	GER	INF
5. We decided to order a pizza.	GER	INF
6. David has discussed quitting his job several times.	GER	INF
7. The police officers planned to work overtime during the conference.	GER	INF
8. Kevin would like to grow organic vegetables in his garden.	GER	INF

PRACTICE 4 ▸ Verb + gerund or infinitive. (Charts 13-1 → 13-3)

Choose the correct completions.

1. I would like   inviting / (to invite)   you and some of my other friends for dinner sometime.

2. I enjoyed   being / to be   with my family at the lake last summer.

3. My parents can't afford   paying / to pay   all my college expenses.

4. Theresa, would you mind   mailing / to mail   this letter on your way home?

5. Do you expect   passing / to pass   this course? If so, you'd better work harder.

6. Mr. Reed refused   considering / to consider   my proposal. He had already made up his mind.

7. I wish he would consider   accepting / to accept   my proposal. I know I can do the job.

8. I don't think I'll ever finish   reading / to read   this report. It just goes on and on.

9. We didn't go   swimming / to swim   last week because it was too cold.

10. I'm really sorry. I didn't mean   hurting / to hurt   your feelings.

11. Why do you keep   asking / to ask   me the same question over and over again?

12. I've decided   looking / to look   for another job. I'll never be happy here.

13. You need   trying / to try   harder if you want to get a promotion.

14. Why do you pretend   enjoying / to enjoy   Leon's company? I know you don't like him.

15. Let's get together tonight. I want to talk about   opening / to open   a new business.

16. I have a secret. Do you promise   keeping / to keep   it to yourself?

17. The director plans   giving / to give   everyone a bonus at the end of the year.

18. I have a good job, and I hope   supporting / to support   myself all through school.

19. I can't wait   finishing / to finish   work today. I'm starting my vacation tonight.

20. I want   visiting / to visit   the pyramids while I'm studying in Cairo.

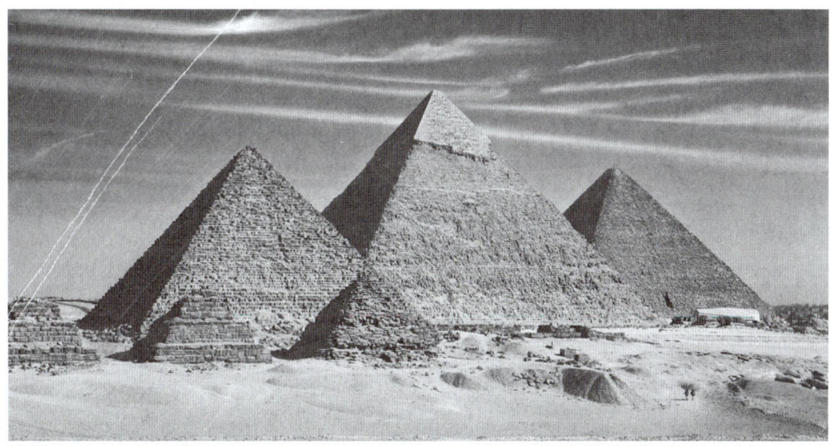

PRACTICE 5 ▸ Verb + gerund or infinitive. (Charts 13-1 → 13-4)
Choose <u>all</u> the correct answers.

1. I want _____ the new movie you've been talking about.

   a. seeing   b. to see

2. I'm a people-watcher. I like _____ people in public places.

   a. watching   b. to watch

3. I've already begun _____ ideas for my new novel.

   a. collecting   b. to collect

4. A group of Chinese scientists plan _____ their discovery at the conference next spring.

   a. presenting   b. to present

5. Whenever I wash my car, it starts _____ .

   a. raining   b. to rain

6. Angela and I continued _____ for several hours.

   a. talking   b. to talk

7. I love _____ on the beach during a storm.

   a. walking   b. to walk

8. I would love _____ a walk today.

   a. taking   b. to take

9. Are you sure you don't mind _____ Johnny for me while I go to the store?

   a. watching   b. to watch

10. Annie hates _____ in the rain.

   a. driving   b. to drive

11. My roommate can't stand _____ to really loud rock music.

   a. listening   b. to listen

12. I don't like _____ in front of other people.

   a. singing   b. to sing

13. Would you like _____ to the concert with us?

   a. going   b. to go

14. Charlie likes to go _____ when the weather is very windy.

   a. sailing   b. to sail

15. Most children can't wait _____ their presents on their birthday.

   a. opening   b. to open

PRACTICE 6 ▸ Verb + gerund or infinitive. (Charts 13-1, 13-3, and 13-4)

Complete the passages with the infinitive or gerund form of the verbs in parentheses.

1. Cindy wants (*go*) _____ *to go* _____ to graduate school next year. However, she can't

   afford (*pay*) _____ all the tuition, so she needs (*get*) _____

   a scholarship. She intends (*apply*) _____ for a scholarship which is given

   to students who have done outstanding work in biology. She is optimistic, and she expects (*receive*)

   _____ it.

2. Carla and Marco are planning (*take*) _____ a vacation. Carla would love

   (*go*) _____ to a tropical beach, but Marco doesn't like hot weather. He prefers

   cold weather and would like (*go*) _____ skiing in the mountains. Although Carla

   prefers hot weather, she doesn't mind (*be*) _____ in cold weather. They will

   probably decide (*go*) _____ to the mountains this year, and Marco will enjoy (*ski*)

   _____ Next year, they'll go to the tropics and go (*swim*) _____ and

   (*sail*) _____ in the warm ocean.

3. Tom Fan was considering (*get*) _____ another job. The job that he has is a good

   one, but it doesn't have opportunities to advance. Tom decided (*tell*) _____ his

   boss, Sharon, that he was thinking about (*leave*) _____ the company because

   he needed (*have*) _____ more opportunities to advance. Sharon offered (*create*)

   _____ a new position for Tom, one with more responsibility. Tom happily

   accepted the offer and agreed (*take*) _____ the new job as regional sales manager

   of a large area.

Complete the sentences with the gerund or infinitive form of the verb. Some verbs may take both.

Part I. Use ***work***.

1. I agreed ______*to work*______.
2. I put off ______*working*______.
3. I would love ________________.
4. I thought about ________________.
5. I promised ________________.
6. I began ________________.

7. I decided ________________.
8. I offered ________________.
9. I quit ________________.
10. I refused ________________.
11. I hoped ________________.
12. I finished ________________.

Part II. Use ***leave***.

13. She expected ________________.
14. She wanted ________________.
15. She considered ________________.
16. She talked about ________________.
17. She postponed ________________.

18. She put off ________________.
19. She refused ________________.
20. She needed ________________.
21. She thought about ________________.
22. She hoped ________________.

Part III. Use ***know***.

23. They seemed ________________.
24. They expected ________________.
25. They would like ________________.
26. They don't mind ________________.
27. They would love ________________.

28. They want ________________.
29. They can't stand ________________.
30. They needed ________________.
31. They appeared ________________.
32. They hated ________________.

Complete the sentences with the correct prepositions. Underline the gerunds.

Part I. Liz …

1. is afraid ______*of*______ flying.
2. apologized ______*for*______ hurting her friend's feelings.
3. believes ______*in*______ helping others.
4. is good ______*at*______ listening to her friends' concerns.
5. is tired ______*of*______ working weekends.
6. is nervous ______*about*______ walking home from work late at night.
7. dreams ______*about*______ owning a farm with horses, cows, and sheep.
8. talks ______*about*______ buying a farm in the country.

Part II. Leo …

9. is responsible ______*for*______ closing the restaurant where he works at night.
10. thanked his father ______*for*______ lending him some money.
11. plans ______*on*______ becoming an accountant.
12. forgave his roommate ______*for*______ taking his car without asking.

13. insists _______on_______ eating only fresh fruits and vegetables.

14. is looking forward _____To_______ finishing school.

15. stopped his best friend _____from_______ making a bad decision.

16. is worried _____about_______ not having enough time for family and friends.

PRACTICE 9 ▸ Preposition + gerund. (Chart 13-5 and C-2)

Complete the sentences. Use prepositions and gerunds.

1. Bill interrupted me. He apologized _____*for*_____ that.

   Bill apologized _____*for interrupting*_____ me.

2. I like to learn about other countries and cultures. I'm interested _________ that.

   I'm interested _______________________ about other countries and cultures.

3. I helped Ann. She thanked me _________ that.

   Ann thanked me _______________________ her.

4. Nadia wanted to walk to work. She insisted _________ that.

   We offered Nadia a ride, but she insisted _______________________ to work.

5. Nick lost my car keys. I forgave him _________ that.

   I forgave Nick _______________________ my car keys when he borrowed my car.

6. Sara wants to go out to eat just because she feels _________ it.

   She feels _______________________ out to eat.

7. I'm not a good artist. I try to draw faces, but I'm not very good _________ it.

   I'm not good _______________________ faces.

8. Mr. and Mrs. Reed have been saving some money for their retirement. They believe _________ that.

   Mr. and Mrs. Reed believe _______________________ money for their retirement.

9. I may forget the words I'm supposed to say in my graduation speech. I'm worried _________ that.

   I'm worried _______________________ the words in my speech.

10. The children are going to go to Disneyland. They're excited _________ that.

    The children are excited _______________________ to Disneyland.

11. Their parents are going to Disneyland too. They are looking forward _________ that.

    Their parents are looking forward _______________________ there too.

12. Max doesn't like to stay in hotels because he is scared of heights. He is afraid _________ that.

    Max is afraid _______________________ in hotels.

13. I didn't study abroad last year, but I thought _________ it.

    I thought _______________________ abroad last year.

14. I don't want to watch another movie tonight. I'm tired of it.

    I'm tired _______________________ movies.

Choose the correct completions for each group.

Part I. Completions with ***ask***.

a. about asking for more money	d. to ask for a few days off
b. about asking the Petersons	e. to ask for directions
c. asking "why"	f. to ask you about a grammar rule

1. A: You look tired, Yoko. Can you stay home from work for a few days?

    B: Yes. I intend ___d___ .

2. A: Sid, we're lost! Why don't you ask someone where the highway is?

    B: You know that I hate ______ .

3. A: You're going to talk to the boss about getting a raise, aren't you?

    B: I don't know. I'm really nervous ______ .

4. A: Who do you want to invite to our holiday party?

    B: I'm thinking ______ .

5. A: Your little girl has a lot of questions, doesn't she?

    B: Yes, she's very curious. She keeps ______ over and over again.

6. A: Yes, do you have a question about the homework?

    B: Yes, I do. I'd like ______ .

    A: Which one?

Part II. Completions with ***fix***.

g. about fixing it	j. to fix everything herself
h. at fixing things	k. to fix it myself
i. for fixing it	l. to fix it tomorrow

7. A: Are you going to fix your mother's car?

    B: No, she doesn't need help. She prefers ______ .

8. A: Are you going to call the technician to fix your computer?

    B: No, I intend ______ right now.

9. A: Is the plumber coming to fix your faucet?

    B: No. My husband promised ______ .

10. A: This sidewalk has been broken for a long time! When is the city going to fix it?

    B: They've been talking ______ for months, but they never do.

11. A: Oh, I'm so sorry! I didn't mean to break your chair.

    B: Don't worry about it. Jerry will fix it. He's excellent ______ .

12. A: My car has a real problem. It's very hard to steer.

    B: Did you know that the company is responsible ______? All the cars have been recalled, and the

    company has to fix them for free.

Choose <u>all</u> the correct completions.

(1) I am a procrastinator. A procrastinator is a person who puts off (doing) / to do something that she hates **doing / to do** until a later time. Unfortunately, although the person may intend **doing / to do** the task soon, it may not be done for a long time.

(2) Here's an example. I received a beautiful silk sweater from my Aunt Sarah. I meant **write / to write** to her immediately to thank her, but I postponed **doing / to do** so. I kept **thinking / to think**, "I'll write tomorrow." After a month, I hadn't written to her, and I was too embarrassed to call her. Finally I wrote this:

Dear Aunt Sarah,

(3) I apologize **for being / to be** so late with this note. I want **to thank / thanking** you for **sending / to send** me the lovely blue silk sweater. I will certainly enjoy **wearing / to wear** it to parties and special events. In fact, I'm planning **wearing / to wear** it to your birthday dinner next week.

(4) I really look forward **to seeing / to see** you then. Please forgive me **for taking / to take** so long to say thank you.

Complete the conversation with the appropriate gerund or infinitive of the word in *italics*. Some sentences also require a preposition.

A: Claire and I are *going* out for lunch this afternoon. Are you interested _______*in going*_______ with us?

B: Sure! I haven't *eaten* all day. I would love __________________ with you and Claire. Where are you
                    1
   going?

A: We haven't *picked* a restaurant yet. Do you want __________________ a place?
                                       2

B: There's a really good Thai restaurant downtown, but it's always crowded. We'll have to *wait* for a
   table. We can go there if you don't mind ________________.
                                         3

A: I don't know. There *is* an important meeting at 2:00. I'm worried ________________ late.
                                           4

B: Then let's *choose* a different restaurant. We need ________________ a place that is nearby and not
                                       5
   very crowded.

A: There's a pizzeria across the street, and it has a fun trivia game that we can *play* while we wait for
   our pizza. You love ________________ trivia, right?
                           6

B: Yes, that's right, but I *had* pizza for dinner last night. I don't really feel like ________________
                                              7
   pizza again.

A: How about the new seafood place on Center Street? It takes about twenty minutes to *walk* there, but
   we can drive instead ________________.
                                  8

B: That sounds great. And by the way, you *paid* for lunch last time we went out, so I insist
   ________________ this time.
                 9

A: Okay, if you insist. Thanks!

Describe what the people did by using **by** + a gerund.

1. MARY: How did you comfort the baby?
   SUE: I held him in my arms.
   Sue comforted the baby ____*by holding*____ him in her arms.

2. PAT: How did you improve your vocabulary?
   NADIA: I read a lot of books.
   Nadia improved her vocabulary ____________ a lot of books.

3. KIRK: How did Grandma entertain the kids?
   SALLY: She told them a story.
   Grandma entertained the kids ____________ them a story.

4. MASAKO: How did you improve your English?
   PEDRO: I watched a lot of movies.
   Pedro improved his English ____________ a lot of movies.

5. JEFFREY: How did you catch up with the bus?
   JIM: I ran as fast as I could.
   Jim caught up with the bus ____________ as fast as he could.

6. MR. LEE: How did you earn your children's respect?
   MR. COY: I treated them with respect at all times.
   Mr. Coy earned his children's respect ____________ them with respect at all times.

PRACTICE 14 ▸ *By + gerund.* (Chart 13-6)

Complete the sentences with **by** + an appropriate verb from the box.

count	follow	look	pour	save	stretch	✓take	work

1. I arrived on time ____*by taking*____ a taxi instead of a bus.

2. I put out the fire ____________ water on it.

3. Giraffes can reach the leaves at the tops of trees ____________ their long necks.

4. I finished writing my final paper ____________ all through the night.

5. Sylvia was able to buy an expensive condominium ____________ her money for four years.

6. I cooked the noodles ____________ the directions on the package.

7. You can find out the temperature in any city in the world ____________ it up online.

8. You can figure out how old a tree is ____________ its rings.

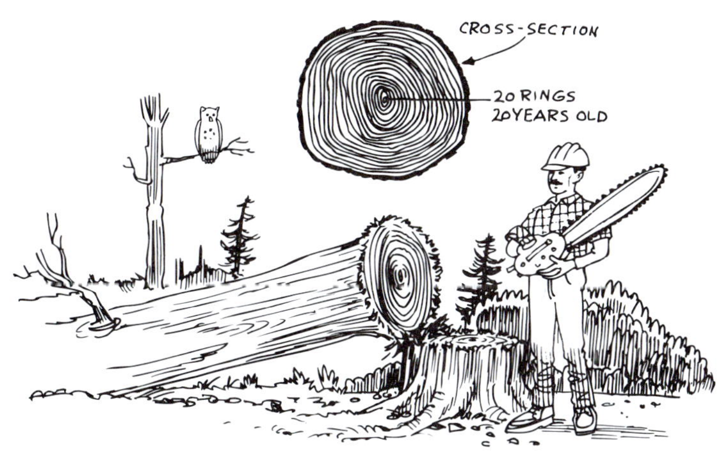

Circle <u>all</u> the correct answers.

1. Ole went to Quebec by ______.
   a. bus
   b. a bus
   c. his feet
   d. plane
   e. taxi
   f. train

2. Kim ate dinner with ______.
   a. a fork
   b. a spoon
   c. chopsticks
   d. fork
   e. hand
   f. knife

3. Ali sent the information by ______.
   a. a phone
   b. email
   c. text
   d. mistake
   e. his hand
   f. phone

4. Sid cleaned the kitchen with ______.
   a. a broom
   b. a mop
   c. hand
   d. soap and water
   e. disinfectant
   f. a cloth

PRACTICE 16 ▶ Gerund as subject; *It* + infinitive. (Chart 13-7)

Complete the sentences by using a gerund as the subject or *it* + infinitive. Add *is* where appropriate. Use the verbs in the box.

complete	eat	live
drive	✓learn	travel

1. a. _____*It is*_____ easy for anyone _____*to learn*_____ how to cook an egg.

   b. _____*Learning*_____ how to cook an egg _____*is*_____ easy for anyone.

2. a. _____*Eating*_____ nutritious food _____*is*_____ important for your health.

   b. _____*It's*_____ important for your health _____*to eat*_____ nutritious food.

3. a. _____*Driving*_____ on the wrong side of the road _____*is*_____ against the law.

   b. _____*It's*_____ against the law _____*To drive*_____ on the wrong side of the road.

4. a. _____*It's*_____ exciting _____*To Travel*_____ to new places.

   b. _____*Traveling*_____ to new places _____*is*_____ exciting.

5. a. _____*Is it*_____ expensive _____*To live*_____ in a dormitory?

   b. _____*Is living*_____ in a dormitory expensive?

6. a. _____*Is it*_____ difficult _____*To complet*_____ these sentences correctly?

   b. _____*Is completing*_____ these sentences correctly difficult?

PRACTICE 17 ▶ Purpose: *to* vs. *for*. (Chart 13-8)

Rewrite the sentences. Use *it … for someone* + an infinitive phrase. Use the adjective in parentheses.

1. Shy people have a hard time meeting others at social events. (*difficult*)

   ___________*It is difficult for shy people to meet*___________ others at social events.

2. In many cultures, young children sleep in the same room as their parents. (*customary*)

   In many cultures, _____*It's customary for young children*_____ in the same room as their parents. *To sleep*

3. Airline pilots need to have good eyesight. (*necessary*)

   ___________*It's necessary for Airline pilot*___________ good eyesight. *To have*

4. Many teenagers can't wake up early. (*hard*)

It's hard for many teenagers to wake up early.

5. Elderly people need to keep their minds active. (*important*)

It's important for elderly people to keep their minds active.

6. People don't like listening to monotone speakers. (*boring*)

It's boring for people to listen to monotone speakers.

7. Scientists will never know the origin of every disease in the world. (*impossible*)

It's impossible for scientists to know the origin of every disease in the world.

PRACTICE 18 ▸ Purpose: *to* vs. *for*. (Chart 13-9)

Complete the sentences with *to* or *for*.

1. Yesterday, I called the doctor's office …

   a. *for* an appointment.
   b. *to* make an appointment.
   c. *to* get a prescription.
   d. *for* a prescription.
   e. *to* ask a question.
   f. *to* get some advice.
   g. *for* some advice.

2. Yesterday, Chuck stayed after class …

   a. *to* talk with the teacher.
   b. *for* a talk with the teacher.
   c. *for* some extra help.
   d. *to* finish a project.
   e. *to* work with other students.
   f. *for* a meeting with other students.
   g. *to* help plan a class party.

PRACTICE 19 ▸ Purpose: *to* vs. *for*. (Chart 13-9)

Complete the sentences with *to* or *for*.

1. We wear coats in cold weather _____*to*_____ keep warm.

2. We wear coats in cold weather _____*for*_____ warmth.

3. Mark contacted a lawyer __________ legal advice.

4. Mark contacted a lawyer __________ discuss a legal problem.

5. Sam went to the hospital __________ an operation.

6. We hired a teenager __________ cut my grandmother's grass twice a month.

7. Frank went to the library __________ review for the test.

8. I play tennis twice a week __________ fun and exercise.

9. Jennifer used some medicine __________ cure an infection on her arm.

10. I lent Yvette some money __________ her school expenses.

11. I asked my manager __________ permission to take the rest of the day off.

PRACTICE 20 ▸ (*In order*) *to*. (Chart 13-9)

Combine the given phrases in *italics* to create sentences using (*in order*) *to*.

1. *watch the news* + *turn on the TV*

   After he got home from work, Jack _____*turned on the TV (in order) to watch the news.*_____

2. *wash his clothes* + *go to the laundromat*

   Every weekend, Martin __________

3. *run + get to class on time*

   Every morning, Jeannette ____

4. *let in some fresh air + open the bedroom windows*

   Every night, I ____

5. *ask them for some money + call his parents*

   Sometimes, Pierre ____

6. *go back to my hometown + visit friends and family*

   Every summer, I ____

7. *study in peace and quiet + go to the library*

   Some evenings, I ____

PRACTICE 21 ▸ *Too* vs. *enough.* (Chart 13-10)

Complete the sentences with the words in parentheses and ***too*** or ***enough***.

1. I have a tight schedule tomorrow, so I can't go to the park.

   a. (*time*) I don't have _____<u>enough time to go</u>_____ to the park.

   b. (*busy*) I'm _____<u>too busy to go</u>_____ to the park.

2. I'm pretty short. I can't touch the ceiling.

   a. (*tall*) I'm not ________________________ to touch the ceiling.

   b. (*short*) I'm ________________________ to touch the ceiling.

3. Marcus has been out of work for months. He can't pay any of his bills.

   a. (*money*) Marcus doesn't have ________________________ to pay his bills.

   b. (*poor*) Marcus is ________________________ to pay his bills.

4. This tea is very hot. I need to wait a while until I can drink it.

   a. (*hot*) This tea is ________________________ to drink.

   b. (*cool*) This tea isn't ________________________ to drink.

5. I feel sick. I don't want to eat anything.

   a. (*sick*) I feel ________________________ to eat anything.

   b. (*well*) I don't feel ________________________ to eat anything.

6. Nora is only six years old. She can't stay home by herself.

   a. (*old*) Nora ________________________ to stay home by herself.

   b. (*young*) Nora ________________________ to stay home by herself.

PRACTICE 22 ▸ *Too* vs. *enough.* (Chart 13-10)

Complete the sentences with ***too, enough***, or ***Ø***.

1. I think this problem is _____Ø_____ important _____enough_____ to require our immediate attention.

2. Nina is not _____too_____ tired _____Ø_____ to finish the project before she goes home.

3. You can do this math problem by yourself. You're _____Ø_____ smart _____enough_____ to figure it out.

4. Our company is _____too_____ small _____Ø_____ to start new branches overseas.

5. My niece doesn't drive yet. She's _____too_____ young _____Ø_____ to get a driver's license.

6. Robert is an amazing runner. His coach thinks he is _________ good _________ to begin training for an Olympic marathon.

7. Look at the children watching the clowns. They can't sit still. They're _________ excited to stay in their chairs.

8. The heat outside is terrible! It's _________ hot _________ to fry an egg on the sidewalk!

PRACTICE 23 ▸ Gerund vs. infinitive. (Chapter 13 Review)

Complete the passage with the correct form of the verbs in parentheses.

Generalizations About Extroverts and Introverts

An extrovert is someone who appears active and confident and who enjoys (*be*)

_________ with other people. This is the opposite of an introvert, who is quiet and
    1

shy and does not want (*spend*) _________ a lot of time with other people.
                                  2

An extrovert gets energy by (*be*) _________ around other people. An introvert
                                      3

gets energy from (*be*) _________ alone.
                        4

Extroverts try (*find*) _________ social situations because they like interacting
                        5

with people. Introverts often avoid (*be*) _________ in social situations because they
                                           6

are not comfortable in them.

An extrovert prefers (*talk*) _________ with someone else instead of (*sit*)
                              7

_________ alone and (*think*) _________. In fact, extroverts
    8   9

sometimes seem (*think*) _________ and speak at the same time, unlike introverts
                        10

who think about their words before (*speak*) _________.
                                              11

Extroverts, are often good at (*make*) _________ social conversation,
                                       12

while introverts — who may be shy at first — would like (*discuss*) _________
                                                                    13

ideas instead.

PRACTICE 24 ▸ Check your knowledge. (Chapter 13 Review)

Correct the errors.

                 to buy
1. I decided not ~~buying~~ a new car.

2. The Johnsons are considering to sell their antique store.

3. Sam finally finished build his vacation home in the mountains.

4. My wife and I go to dancing at the community center every Saturday night.

5. Suddenly, it began to raining, and the wind started to blew.

6. The baby is afraid be away from her mother for any length of time.

7. I am excited for start college this September.

8. You can send your application with email.

9. My country is too beautiful.

10. Is exciting to drive a sports car.

11. My grandparents enjoy to traveling across the country in a motor home.

12. Elena made this sweater with her hands.

13. Running it is one of the sports we can participate in at school.

14. Swim with a group of people is more enjoyable than swim alone.

15. Meeting new people it is interesting.

PRACTICE 25 ▸ Gerunds and infinitives. (Chapter 13 Review)

Complete the sentences with the gerund or infinitive form of the verbs in parentheses.

1. (*study*) _______*Studying*_______ English can be fun.

2. My boss makes a habit of (*write*) ____________________

   nice messages to her employees when they've done a

   good job.

3. A: Do you think that it's important for kids (*have*)

   ____________________ chores around the house?

   B: Yes, I do. I think it's essential for them (*learn*)

   ____________________ about responsibility that way.

4. A: I don't like airplanes.

   B: Why? Are you afraid of (*fly*) ____________________?

   A: No, I'm afraid of (*crash*) ____________________.

5. A: Let's quit (*argue*) ____________________. Let's just agree (*disagree*)

   ____________________. We can still be friends.

   B: Sounds good to me. And I apologize for (*raise*) ____________________ my voice. I didn't

   mean (*yell*) ____________________ at you.

   A: That's okay. I didn't intend (*get*) ____________________ angry at you either.

6. A: What do you feel like (*do*) ____________________ this afternoon?

   B: I feel like (*go*) ____________________ (*shop*) ____________________ at the mall. What

   about you?

   A: I don't mind (*shop*) ____________________ at the mall when it's quiet, but there's a sale today

   and it will be too crowded.

7. A: Have you called Alexa yet?

   B: No, I keep (*put*) ____________________ it off.

A: Why?

B: She's mad at me for (*forget*) _________________ (*send*) _________________ her a

card on her birthday.

8. From the earth, the sun and the moon appear (*be*) _________________ almost the same size.

PRACTICE 26 ▸ Crossword puzzle. (Chapter 13 Review)

Complete the puzzle. Use the clues to find the correct words. All are grammar points from Chapter 13.

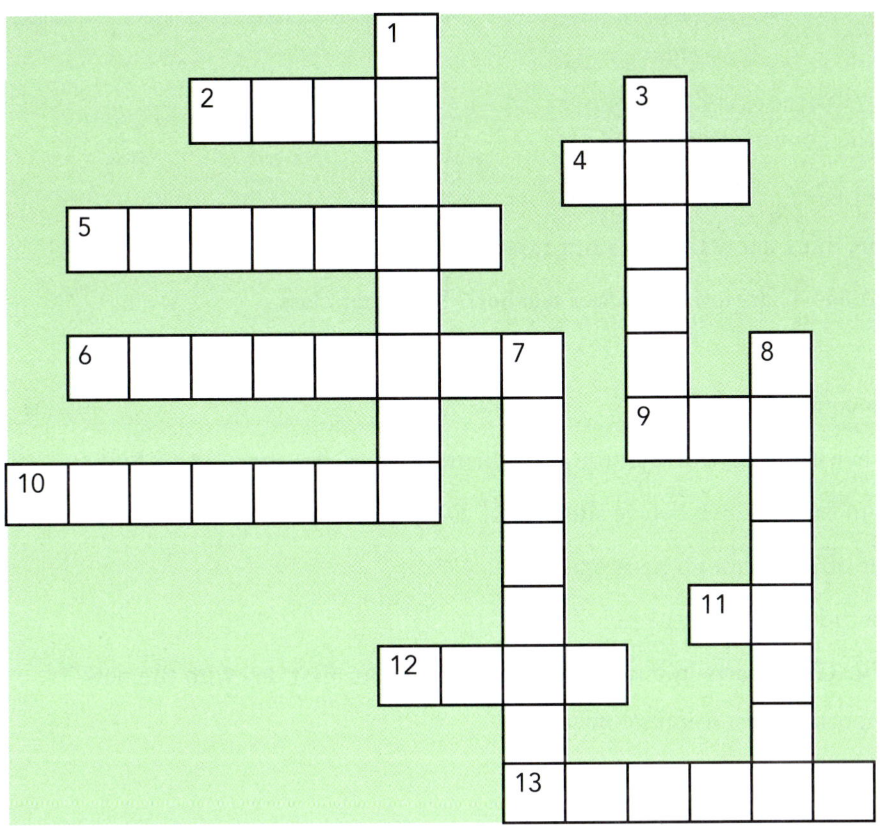

Across

2. The best way to eat pizza is _________________ your fingers.

4. Sorry! I am _________________ tired to go out tonight.

5. Would you mind _________________ me up for work tomorrow? My car is being fixed.

6. Ben buys things at the mall on weekends when he goes _________________.

9. We went to the lecture early in order to _________________ good seats.

10. My family and I enjoy _________________ together in our small sailboat.

11. The only way to get to the small island is _________________ boat.

12. It's not difficult for Carlos to _________________ the guitar because he is a professional guitarist.

13. Bob is 21. He is old _________________ to vote.

Down

1. We are considering _________________ our vacation plans. We may go in July instead of in June.

3. The Stein family is thinking about _________________ to a larger house.

7. Margo expects to _________________ from college next June.

8. I finished _________________ at midnight and went right to bed.

PRACTICE 1 ▸ Noun clauses: introduction. (Chart 14-1)

Underline the noun clauses in the conversation.

A: Do you know who that man is?

B: Yes. I don't know his name, but I know that he's our new grammar teacher.

A: Really? What happened to Ms. Clarkson, our other teacher? I love her class.

B: She's moving to Alaska.

A: Do you know why she's moving to Alaska?

B: I'm not sure. I know that her husband works in the oil industry. Maybe he got a job in Alaska.

A: I'll really miss her. I want to say goodbye before she leaves. Do you know if she's still here?

B: Yes, she is. I saw her in her office about an hour ago.

A: Great! I'm going to run to there now and see her.

B: Okay, but you should hurry. Class starts in ten minutes, and this is our first day with the new

teacher. You know how important first impressions are.

PRACTICE 2 ▸ Questions vs. noun clauses. (Chart 14-2)

If the sentence contains a noun clause, <u>underline</u> it and circle "noun clause". If the question word introduces a question, circle "question". Add appropriate final punctuation: a period (.) or a question mark (?).

1. I don't know where Yuri lives.	**noun clause**	question
2. Where does Yuri live?	noun clause	**question**
3. I don't understand why Sofia left	noun clause	question
4. Why did Sofia leave	noun clause	question
5. When did Oliver leave	noun clause	question
6. I don't know when Oliver left	noun clause	question
7. What does "calm" mean	noun clause	question
8. Tarik knows what "calm" means	noun clause	question
9. I don't know how long the earth has existed	noun clause	question
10. How long has the earth existed	noun clause	question
11. Where is Patagonia	noun clause	question
12. I don't know where Patagonia is	noun clause	question

Answer the questions using noun clauses.

1. A: Where does Helen work?
   B: I don't know where _____*Helen works*_____.

2. A: What did Adam say?
   B: I didn't hear what _____*Adam said*_____.

3. A: Why are we doing this?
   B: I don't know why _____*we are doing this*_____.

4. A: When does the new semester start?
   B: Tell me when _____*the we semester start*_____.

5. A: Where did everyone go?
   B: I don't know where _____*everyone went*_____.

6. A: How late is the gym open?
   B: I don't know how late _____*the gym is open*_____.

7. A: Who believes that story?
   B: I don't know who _____*believes that story*_____.

8. A: Whose phone is ringing?
   B: I don't know whose _____*phone is ringing*_____.

Complete the noun clauses. Add appropriate final punctuation: a period (.) or a question mark (?).

1. Vince doesn't live near me. Do you know where _____*Vince lives?*_____
2. I've never seen that woman. I don't know who _____*that woman is.*_____
3. Henri dropped something. Do you know what _____
4. I don't know her phone number. Do you know what _____
5. These are someone's keys. I don't know whose _____
6. Clara met someone. Do you know who _____
7. Carlo is absent today. I don't know why _____
8. What time is it? Do you know what time _____
9. Sam is studying something. Do you know what _____
10. Someone sent Amy flowers. Do you know who _____
11. Ms. Gray will call later today. Do you know when _____
12. The president is going to say something. We don't know what _____
13. Who is in that room? Do you know who _____
14. What is in that drawer? Does anyone know what
    _____

15. A 3D printer costs a lot of money, doesn't it?
    Do you know how much _____

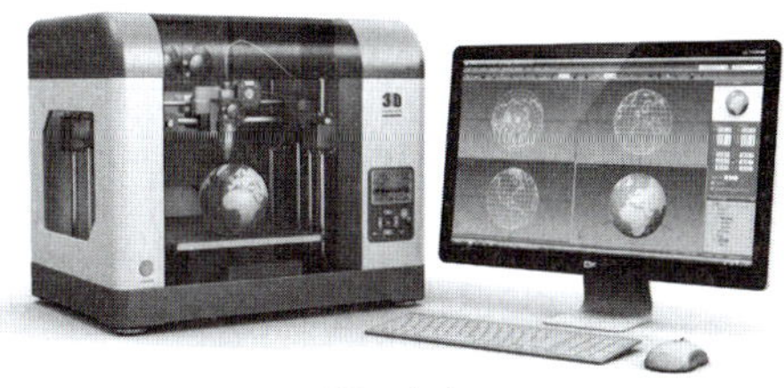

3D printer

PRACTICE 5 ▸ Information questions and noun clauses. (Chart 14-2)
Complete the question and noun clause forms of the given sentences.

1. Marcos left at 11:00.

   When ______*did Marcos leave?*______

   Could you tell me ______*when Marcos left?*______

2. He said good-bye.

   What ___________________________

   I didn't hear ___________________________

3. The post office is on Second Street.

   Where ___________________________

   Could you please tell me ___________________________

4. It's half-past six.

   What time ___________________________

   Could you please tell me ___________________________

5. David arrived two days ago.

   When ___________________________

   I don't know ___________________________

6. Ana is from Peru.

   What country ___________________________

   I'd like to know ___________________________

7. Kathy was absent because she was ill.

   Why ___________________________ absent?

   Do you know ___________________________ absent?

8. Pedro lives next door.

   Who ___________________________ next door?

   Do you know ___________________________ next door?

9. Someone's car is in the driveway.

   Whose ___________________________ in the driveway?

   Do you know ___________________________ in the driveway?

10. These books are someone's.

    Whose ___________________________

    Do you know ___________________________

11. Emma has studied English for five years.

    How long ___________________________

    I'm not sure ___________________________

12. Jesse exercises five days a week.

    How often ___________________________

    I really don't know ___________________________

Complete each sentence with a noun clause made from the words in *italics*. There is one extra word in each list.

1. *who, to, did, Helen, talked*

   Who did Helen talk to? Do you know ______*who Helen talked to*______?

2. *does, who, lives*

   Who lives in that apartment? Do you know _________________________ in that apartment?

3. *he, what, said, did*

   What did he say? Tell me _________________________.

4. *has, Pat, does, what kind of car*

   What kind of car does Pat have? I can't remember _________________________.

5. *how, their kids, are, old, do*

   How old are their kids? I can't ever remember _________________________.

6. *why, did, you, said*

   Why did you say that? I don't understand _________________________ that.

7. *I, do, can, catch, where*

   Where can I catch the bus? Could you please tell me _________________________ the bus?

8. *does, what, this word, means*

   What does this word mean? Could you please tell me _________________________?

PRACTICE 7 ▸ Noun clauses. (Chart 14-2)

Choose the correct answers.

1. A: Why ______ so late?

      a. is Jeff   b. Jeff is

   B: I'm not sure why ______ late today. He's almost always late.

      a. he is   b. is he

2. A: Tell us where ______ on your vacation, Pam.

      a. you went   b. did you go

   B: I went sailing in the Bahamas. Where ______ on your vacation?

      a. you went   b. did you go

3. A: I couldn't understand the professor. What ______?

      a. she said   b. did she say

   B: I couldn't understand her either. I have no idea what ______.

      a. she said   b. did she say

4. A: What ______?

      a. this word means   b. does this word mean

   B: I don't know what ______.

      a. it means   b. does it mean

5. A: Who _____ on the phone?

    a. was that   b. that was

  B: I don't know who _____. The person hung up.

    a. was that   b. that was

6. A: Do you know what _____?

    a. a bumblebee is   b. is a bumblebee

  B: Ask Helen. She knows a lot of words. Hey, Helen. What _____?

    a. a bumblebee is   b. is a bumblebee

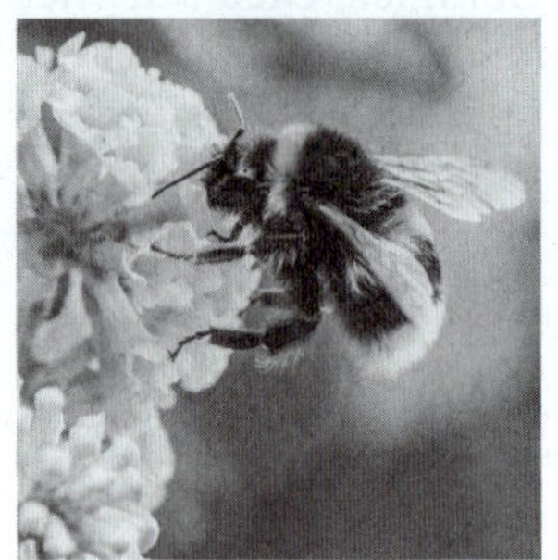

A bumblebee

PRACTICE 8 ▸ Noun clauses. (Chart 14-2)

Read the email message. Choose the correct completion in each pair.

Hi Mom and Dad:

(1) Well, after one week in Mexico, I'm happy to be here, but I also feel a little lost at times. I thought that I knew some Spanish, but really, I can't understand what **people are saying / are people saying**. Even though I have a map, I can't read it very well, so I don't know where **are all the buildings / all the buildings are**. I know when **my classes start / do my classes start** — next Monday — and where **I register / do I register**. I know what classes **am I taking / I am taking**, but I don't know who **my professors will be / will be my professors**.

(2) Last night I felt lonely. I don't know how long **it will take / will it take** to make new friends, and I was wondering why **did I come / I came** here. But today I feel much better, and I know why **am I / I am** here: I'm going to study another language and learn about another culture, and I'm going to be making new friends.

Love, Pat ☺

PRACTICE 9 ▸ Noun clauses that begin with *if* or *whether*. (Chart 14-3)

Change each question to a noun clause.

1. YES/NO QUESTION: Is Tom coming?

   NOUN CLAUSE: I wonder _____ *if / whether Tom is coming* _____.

2. YES/NO QUESTION: Has Jin finished medical school yet?

   NOUN CLAUSE: I don't know _if Jin has finished medical school yet_.

3. YES/NO QUESTION: Does Daniel have any time off soon?

   NOUN CLAUSE: I don't know _if Daniel has any time off soon_.

4. YES/NO QUESTION: Is the flight on time?

   NOUN CLAUSE: Can you tell me _if the flight is on time_?

5. YES/NO QUESTION: Is there enough gas in the car?

   NOUN CLAUSE: Do you know _if there is enough gas in the car_?

6. YES/NO QUESTION: Is Yuki married?

   NOUN CLAUSE: I can't remember _if Yuki is married_ .

7. YES/NO QUESTION: Are the Nelsons going to move?

   NOUN CLAUSE: I wonder _if the Nelsons are going to move_ .

8. YES/NO QUESTION: Did Khaled change jobs?

   NOUN CLAUSE: I don't know _if Khaled changed jobs._ .

PRACTICE 10 ▸ Noun clauses. (Chart 14-3)

Complete the sentences with the correct form of the verbs. Pay special attention to the use of final **-s/-es**.

1. Does it rain a lot here?

   Could you tell me if it ______ _rains_ ______ a lot here?

2. How hot does it get in the summer?

   Could you tell me how hot it ______ _gets_ ______ in the summer?

3. What do people like to do here?

   Could you tell me what people ______ _like_ ______ to do here?

4. Does bus number 10 run on holidays?

   Could you tell me if bus number 10 ______ _runs_ ______ on holidays?

5. Do the buses run on holidays?

   Could you tell me if the buses ______ _run_ ______ on holidays?

6. How long does it take to get to the city?

   Could you tell me how long it ______ _takes_ ______ to get to the city?

7. What do people enjoy most about this area?

   Could you tell me what people ______ _enjoy_ ______ most about this area?

8. Does it seem like an expensive place to live?

   Could you tell me if it ______ _seems_ ______ like an expensive place to live?

PRACTICE 11 ▸ Noun clauses with questions. (Charts 14-2 and 14-3)

Complete the sentences using noun clauses.

1. A: Are you going to need help moving furniture to your new apartment?

   B: I don't know ______ _if I'm going to need_ ______ help. Thanks for asking. I'll let you know.

2. A: I'm going to try the fish tacos. What are you going to order?

   A: I can't decide _what you are going to order_. I need a few more minutes.

3. A: Will there be a live band at this restaurant tonight?

   B: I'll ask the server. Excuse me, we're wondering _if there'll be_ a live band
      here tonight.

4. A: Where do birds go in hurricanes?

   B: That's a good question. I have no idea _where birds go_ in hurricanes.

5. A: Can I borrow the car, Dad?

   B: I'll tell you later _if you can borrow_ the car.

6. A: Why did Harold leave town so fast?

   B: I really don't know _________________________ town so fast.

PRACTICE 12 ▶ *That*-clauses. (Chart 14-4)
Choose the correct answers.

1. Johnny's hungry. I guess that _____ .

2. Why are you afraid to fly on planes? Read this report. It proves that _____ .

3. Our son has nightmares. He often dreams that _____ .

4. The police assume that _____ .

5. I have to get up very early tomorrow, so I suppose _____ .

6. I always know when Paul is nervous. Have you ever noticed that _____ ?

7. I used to think that older people couldn't learn a new language, but now I realize that _____ .

8. I'm not sure about the benefits of coffee, but I know that _____ .

a. monsters are chasing him

b. he always bites his fingernails when he is anxious

c. he didn't eat much lunch

d. they can

e. green tea has some healthy ingredients

f. flying is a lot safer than driving

g. an experienced thief stole the money

h. I should go to bed early tonight

PRACTICE 13 ▶ *That*-clauses. (Charts 14-4 and 14-5)
Add *that* to the sentences at the appropriate places to mark the beginning of a noun clause.

1. I'm sorry ^*that* you won't be here for Joe's party.

2. I predict Jim and Sue will get married before the end of the year.

3. I'm surprised you sold your car.

4. Are you certain Mr. McVay won't be here tomorrow?

5. Did you notice Marco shaved off his mustache?

6. It's a fact hot air rises.

7. A: How do you know it's going to be nice tomorrow?

   B: I heard the weather report.

   A: So? The weather report is often wrong, you know. I'm still worried it'll rain on our picnic.

8. A: I heard Professor Samson is leaving the university.

   B: Really? Why?

   A: Some people assume he is going to retire. But I doubt it. I think he is going to do research and writing.

   B: This is not good news! He's a great teacher.

Write two sentences for each passage. Make noun clauses and include the words in parentheses.

1. The Jensens celebrated the graduation of their granddaughter Alice from the university. After graduation, she was offered a good job in chemical research in a nearby town.

   The Jensens (*be pleased*) _____ *are pleased that their granddaughter graduated from the university* _____.

   They (*be glad*) _____ *are glad that she was offered a good job* _____.

2. One night on the news, Joe's parents heard about a big fire at Joe's university. All the students had to leave their dorms. Joe's parents thought that maybe Joe had been injured. When Joe called them about an hour later, they felt relieved.

   At first, Joe's parents (*be worried*) _____ were worried that Joe had been injured. _____.

   Then, they (*be happy*) _____ were happy because Joe called them. _____.

3. Kyle didn't study for his math exam. Afterward, he thought he had failed, but actually, he got one of the highest grades in the class. His teacher had known he would do well and praised him for earning such a high grade.

   Kyle (*be afraid*) _____ was afraid that he had low score in his math exam. _____.

   Kyle's teacher (*not, be surprised*) _____ wasn't surprised that Kyle has receive high school. _____.

4. Karen lent her cousin Mark some money. He said that he needed it to pay the rent. Then she heard that he had bought an expensive new phone. She feels upset that Mark lied to her. She regrets lending him money.

   Karen (*be angry*) _____ was angry that Mark lied to her. _____.

   Karen (*be sorry*) _____ was sorry that she lent Mark the money. _____.

5. People used to think that strenuous exercise was bad for the heart. However, now scientists have proven the opposite: strenuous exercise can be good for the heart. In addition, people used to think that eating a lot of red meat was good for the heart. Now doctors know that eating a lot of red meat is bad for the heart.

   It is a fact (*exercise*) _____ that strenuous exercise is good for the heart _____.

   It is true (*eating a lot of red meat*) _____ that eating a lot of red meat is not bad for the heart _____.

Give the meaning of *so* by writing a *that*-clause.

1. A: Does Alice have a car?

   B: I don't think *so*. (= I don't think _____ *that Alice has a car* _____.)

2. A: Is the library open on Sunday?

   B: I believe *so*. (= I believe _____.)

3. A: Does Ann speak Spanish?

   B: I don't think *so*. (= I don't think _____.)

4. A: Did Alex pass his French course?

   B: I think *so*. (= I think _____.)

5. A: Is Mr. Kozari going to be at the meeting?

   B: I hope *so*. (= I hope _____.)

6. A: Are these pants clean?

   B: I believe *so*. (= I believe _____.)

PRACTICE 16 ▸ Quoted speech. (Chart 14-7)

All the sentences contain quoted speech. Punctuate them by adding quotation marks ("…"),
commas (,), periods (.), and question marks (?). Use capital letters as necessary.

Example: My roommate said the door is open could you close it

My roommate said, **"The door is open. Could you close it?"**

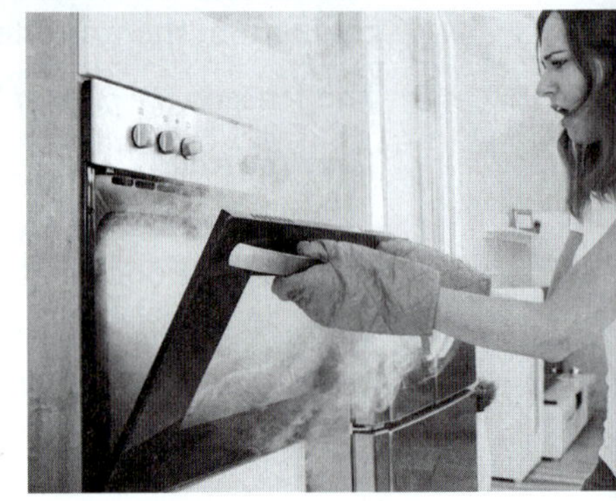

1. Alex asked do you smell smoke

2. Something is burning he said

3. He asked do you smell smoke something is burning

4. Do you smell smoke he asked something is burning

5. Eva said I burned my dinner

6. I burned my dinner I'll have to fix something else she said

7. She said I burned my dinner I'll have to fix something else what should I have

PRACTICE 17 ▸ Quoted speech. (Charts 14-7 and 14-8)

Punctuate the quoted passage. Add quotation marks ("…"), commas (,), periods (.), and question
marks (?). Use capital letters as necessary.

One day my friend Laura and I were sitting in her apartment. We were having a cup of tea
together and talking about the terrible earthquake that had just occurred in Iran. Laura asked me,
"Have you ever been in an earthquake?"

Yes, I have I replied.

Was it a big earthquake she asked.

I've been in several earthquakes, and they've all been small ones I answered. Have you ever been
in an earthquake?

There was an earthquake in my village five years ago Laura said. I was in my house. Suddenly
the ground started shaking. I grabbed my little brother and ran outside. Everything was moving. I was
scared to death. And then suddenly it was over.

I'm glad you and your brother weren't hurt I said.

Yes, we were very lucky. Has everyone in the world felt an earthquake sometime in their lives
Laura wondered. Do earthquakes occur everywhere on the earth?

Those are interesting questions I said but I don't know the answers.

PRACTICE 18 ▸ Reported speech: changing pronouns and possessive words. (Chart 14-8)

Complete the sentences with the correct pronouns or possessive words.

1. Mr. Lee said, "I'm not happy with my new assistant."

   Mr. Lee said that _____*he*_____ wasn't happy with _____*his*_____ new assistant.

2. Tom said to his wife, "My parents invited us over for dinner next weekend."

   Tom said that _________________ parents had invited _________________ over for dinner
   next weekend.

3. Emma said, "I can't find my favorite shoes."

   Emma said that _________________ couldn't find _________________ favorite shoes.

4. Jim said, "A police officer gave Anna and me tickets for jaywalking and told us to cross the street with the traffic lights at the pedestrian crosswalk."

   Jim said that a police officer had given Anna and _______________ tickets for jaywalking and told _______________ to cross the street with the traffic lights at the crosswalk.

5. The Johnsons said to me, "We will send you an email when we arrive in Nepal."

   The Johnsons said that _______________ would send _______________ an email when _______________ arrived in Nepal.

6. Jane said, "I want my daughter to feel good about herself."

   Jane said that _______________ wanted _______________ daughter to feel good about herself.

7. Mary and Jack said to me, "We are going to be out of town on the day of your party."

   Mary and Jack said that _______________ were going to be out of town on the day of _______________ party.

8. Bob said to us, "We will join you after we take my mother to the airport."

   Bob told us that _______________ would join _______________ after _______________ took _______________ mother to the airport.

PRACTICE 19 ▸ Verb forms in reported speech. (Chart 14-9)

Complete each sentence with the correct form of the verb.

1. Juan said, "I will meet you at the corner of Fifth and Broadway."

   Formal: Juan said (that) he ___*would meet*___

   Informal: Juan said (that) he ___*will meet*___ us at the corner of Fifth and Broadway.

2. Maria said, "I'm going to be about 15 minutes late for work."

   Formal: Maria said she _______________

   Informal: Maria said she _______________ about 15 minutes late for work.

3. Roberto said, "My new car has a dent."

   Formal: Roberto said his new car _______________

   Informal: Roberto said his new car _______________ a dent.

4. Phil said, "I need to borrow some money."

   Formal: Phil said he _______________

   Informal: Phil said he _______________ to borrow some money.

5. Sandy said, "I have flown on an airplane only once."

   Formal: Sandy said she _______________

   Informal: Sandy said she _______________ on an airplane only once.

6. Sami and Jun said, "We are planning a surprise party for Naoko."

   Formal: Sami and Jun said they _______________

   Informal: Sami and Jun said they _______________ a surprise party for Naoko.

7. Naoko said, "I don't want any gifts for my birthday."

Formal: Naoko said she ________________ any gifts for her birthday.

Informal: Naoko said she ________________

8. Ms. Wall said, "I can take care of your kids next weekend."

Formal: Ms. Wall said she ________________ of my kids next weekend.

Informal: Ms. Wall said she ________________

PRACTICE 20 ▸ Verb forms in reported speech. (Chart 14-9)

Complete the sentences. Write the opposite of the quoted speech. Use formal sequence of tenses.

1. A: I have a lot of time.

   B: Oh? I misunderstood you. I thought you said _____*(that) you didn't have*_____ a lot of time.

2. A: I found my credit cards.

   B: I misunderstood you. I thought you said ________________ your credit cards.

3. A: The Smiths didn't cancel their party.

   B: I misunderstood you. I thought you said ________________ their party.

4. A: It will rain tomorrow.

   B: I misunderstood you. I thought you said ________________ tomorrow.

5. A: The Whites didn't get a new car.

   B: I misunderstood you. I thought you said ________________ a new car.

6. A: Mei exercises every day.

   B: I misunderstood you. I thought you said ________________ every day.

7. A: My computer is working.

   B: I misunderstood you. I thought you said ________________ .

8. A: Ali isn't coming on Friday.

   B: I misunderstood you. I thought you said ________________ on Friday.

PRACTICE 21 ▸ Reporting questions. (Chart 14-10)

Change the quoted questions to reported questions. Use formal sequence of tenses.

1. Eric said to me, "How old are you?"

   Eric asked me _____*how old I was*_____ .

2. Ms. Rush said to Mr. Long, "Are you going to be at the meeting?"

   Ms. Rush asked Mr. Long _____*if he was going to be*_____ at the meeting.

3. Larry said to Ms. Soo, "Do you have time to help me?"

   Larry asked Ms. Soo ________________ time to help him.

4. Don said to Robert, "Did you change your mind about going to college?"

   Don asked Robert ________________ mind about going to college.

5. Igor said to me, "How long have you been a teacher?"

   Igor asked me ________________ a teacher.

6. I said to Tina, "Can you speak Swahili?"

   I asked Tina ________________ Swahili.

7. Kathy said to Mr. May, "Will you be in your office around three?"

   Kathy asked Mr. May _________________________ around three.

8. The teacher said to Ms. Chang, "Why are you laughing?"

   The teacher asked Ms. Chang _________________________ .

9. My uncle said to me, "Have you ever considered a career in business?"

   My uncle asked me _________________________ a career in business.

PRACTICE 22 ▶ Quoting questions. (Chart 14-10)

Change the reported speech to quotations.

1. Eric asked me if I had ever gone skydiving.

   Eric asked, _____*"Have you ever gone skydiving?"*_________________________

2. Chris wanted to know if I would be at the meeting.

   Chris asked, _________________________

3. Kate wondered whether I was going to quit my job.

   Kate asked, _________________________

4. Anna asked her friend where his car was.

   Anna asked, _________________________

5. Brian asked me what I had done after class yesterday.

   Brian asked, _________________________

6. Luigi asked me if I knew Italian.

   Luigi asked, _________________________

7. Debra wanted to know if I could pick up her daughter at school.

   Debra asked, _________________________

8. My boss wanted to know why I wasn't working at my dcsk.

   My boss asked me, _________________________

PRACTICE 23 ▶ Reported speech. (Charts 14-9 → 14-10)

Complete the reported speech sentences. Use formal sequence of tenses.

1. David said to me, "I'm going to call you on Friday."

   David said _____*(that) he was going to call me*_________________________ on Friday.

2. John said to Ann, "I have to talk to you."

   John told Ann _________________________ .

3. Diane said to me, "I can meet you after work."

   Diane said _________________________ after work.

4. Maria said to Bob, "I wrote you a note."

   Maria told Bob _________________________ a note.

5. Anita asked Mike, "When will I see you again?"

   Anita asked Mike when _________________________ again.

6. Laura said to George, "What are you doing?"

   Laura asked George _________________________ .

PRACTICE 24 ▸ Reporting questions. (Charts 14-9 → 14-10)

A new student, Kenzo, joined an English class. The teacher asked the students to interview him. Here is the list of interview questions.

1. Why did you come here?

2. Have you met many people?

3. What are you going to study?

4. How long will you stay?

5. How do you like it here?

6. Where are you from?

7. Are the local people friendly to you?

8. How did you choose this school?

9. Do you like the weather here?

Later, Kenzo told his friend about the interview. Change the interview questions to noun clauses. Use verbs that are appropriate for later reporting.

1. They asked me ______*why I had to come here.*______________________________

2. They asked me ____

3. They asked me ____

4. They asked me ____

5. They asked me ____

6. They asked me ____

7. They asked me ____

8. They asked me ____

9. They asked me ____

PRACTICE 25 ▸ Reported speech to direct speech. (Charts 14-9 → 14-10)

Complete the sentences using reported speech.

1. Our teacher said that we would have an important exam next week.

   Our teacher said, ______*"You will have an important exam next week."*______________

2. He said that we should take careful notes this week to study for the exam.

   He said ____

3. Julie said that she would be absent tomorrow.

   Julie said ____

4. She explained that she had a doctor's appointment.

   She explained ____

5. She said she was worried about missing the lecture.

   She said ____

6. She asked if she could borrow my notes from class.

   She asked ____

7. I replied that I had to be absent tomorrow too.

   I replied ____

8. Chris told us that he was going to send us both a copy of his notes tomorrow.

   Chris said to Julie ____

PRACTICE 26 ▸ *Say* vs. *tell* vs. *ask.* (Chart 14-10)
Complete the sentences with *said*, *told*, or *asked*.

1. Ava ______*told*______ me that she was hungry.

2. Ava ______*said*______ that she was hungry.

3. Ava ______________ me if I wanted to go out to lunch with her.

4. When the storm began, I ______________ the children to come into the house.

5. When I talked to Mr. Grant, he ______________ he would be at the meeting.

6. Ali ______________ his friends that he had won a scholarship to college. His friends ______________

   they weren't surprised.

7. My supervisor ______________ me if I could postpone my vacation. I ______________ him what

   the reason was. He ______________ that our sales department needed me for a project.

8. My neighbor and I had a disagreement. I ______________ my neighbor that he was wrong.

   My neighbor ______________ me that I was wrong.

9. Fumiko ______________ the teacher that Fatima wasn't going to be in class.

10. Ellen ______________ if I could join her for a movie. I ______________ I wasn't feeling well, but I

    ______________ her what movie she was going to. The next day, Ellen ______________ me she had

    enjoyed the movie.

PRACTICE 27 ▸ Reported speech. (Charts 14-1 → 14-10)
Complete the sentences by changing the quoted speech to reported speech. Use *said*, *told*, *asked*, or
replied. Practice using the formal sequence of tenses.

1. Alex said, "Where do you live?" Alex ______*asked me where I lived.*______

2. He said, "Do you live in the dorm?" He ______________ in the dorm.

3. I said, "I have my own apartment." I ______________ my own apartment.

4. He said, "I'm looking for a new apartment." He ______________ for a new apartment.

5. He said, "I don't like living in the dorm." He ______________ in the dorm.

6. I said, "Do you want to move in with me?" I ______________

7. He said, "Where is your apartment?" He ______________

8. I said, "I live on Seventh Avenue." I ______________ on Seventh Avenue.

9. He said, "But I can't move   He ___________________________

   until the end of May."   until the end of May.

10. He said, "I will cancel my dorm contract   He ___________________________

   at the end of May."   dorm contract at the end of May.

11. He said, "Is that okay?"   He ___________________________

12. I said, "I'm looking forward to having you   I ___________________________

   as a roommate."   as a roommate.

PRACTICE 28 ▶ Reported speech. (Charts 14-1 → 14-10)

Check (✓) all the correct sentences.

1. _______ a. The teacher asked are you finished?

   __✓__ b. The teacher asked if I was finished.

   _______ c. The teacher asked if was I finished?

   _______ d. The teacher asked that I was finished?

   __✓__ e. The teacher asked, "Are you finished?"

2. _______ a. Aki said he was finished.

   _______ b. Aki said that he was finished.

   _______ c. Aki replied that he was finished.

   _______ d. Aki answered that he was finished.

   _______ e. Aki said whether was he finished.

3. _______ a. Ann told Tom, she needed more time.

   _______ b. Ann told Tom she needed more time.

   _______ c. Ann told to Tom she needed more time.

   _______ d. Ann told she needed more time.

   _______ e. Ann said Tom she needed more time.

   _______ f. Ann said she needed more time.

4. _______ a. Donna answered that she was ready.

   _______ b. Donna answered was she ready.

   _______ c. Donna replied ready.

   _______ d. Donna answered, "I am ready."

   _______ e. Donna answered if she was ready.

5. _______ a. Mr. Wong wanted to know if Ted was coming.

   _______ b. Mr. Wong wanted to know is Ted coming?

   _______ c. Mr. Wong wondered if Ted was coming.

   _______ d. Mr. Wong wondered was Ted coming.

   _______ e. Mr. Wong wondered, "Is Ted coming?"

Part I. Read the fable by Aesop.★

> **The Ant and the Grasshopper**
>
> (1–2) In a field one summer day, a grasshopper was jumping around and thinking to himself, "It's a beautiful day, and I love playing in the sun."
>
> (3) An ant passed by. The Ant was carrying a heavy piece of corn.
>
> (4–5) The Grasshopper asked the Ant, "What are you doing and where are you going?"
>
> (6) The Ant replied, "I am carrying food to my nest."
>
> (7–8) The Grasshopper asked "Why are you working so hard in the beautiful weather?"
>
> (9) The Ant said, "If I bring food to the nest in the summer, I can have food in the winter."
>
> (10–11) The Grasshopper asked the Ant, "Can you take a break now and play with me instead of working?"
>
> (12) The Ant answered, "I can't."
>
> (13–14) The Ant said, "If I don't bring food to the nests in the summer, I won't have any food for the winter."
>
> (15) The Grasshopper said, "I'm not worried about the winter because I have plenty of food."
>
> (16–17) The Ant continued walking. The Grasshopper saw many ants doing the same thing. They were carrying heavy loads of food on their backs, and they were all going back to their nests.
>
> (18) The Grasshopper wondered, "Do those ants ever have any fun?"
>
> (19–22) The Grasshopper continued to play in the beautiful weather, and he played all summer long. When winter came, the Grasshopper had no food. In fact, he was getting hungrier and hungrier. The Grasshopper saw the ants. They were eating all the corn and grain that they had collected during the summer.
>
> (23–24) Then the Grasshopper thought to himself, "The ants are smart because they prepared for the winter."
>
> (25–26) And just before the Grasshopper died, he said to himself, "It is always a good idea to prepare for the future."

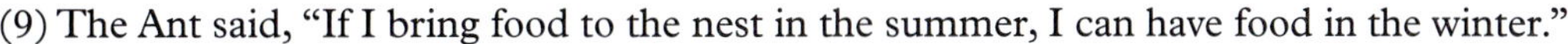

Part II. Complete the sentences by changing the quoted speech to indirect speech. Use formal sequence of tenses.

1. (Lines 1–2) The Grasshopper was thinking to himself ______ *that it was a beautiful day, and that* ______ *he loved playing in the sun* ______.

2. (Line 4) The Grasshopper asked the Ant ______ *what he was doing and* ______

    ______.

3. (Line 6) The Ant replied ______

    ______.

4. (Lines 7–8) The Grasshopper asked the Ant ______

    ______.

★A fable teaches a lesson about right or wrong. Aesop was a Greek writer who wrote many fables.

5. (Line 9) The Ant said ____________________________________

____.

6. (Lines 10–11) The Grasshopper asked the Ant __________________

____.

7. (Line 12) The Ant answered __________________________________.

8. (Lines 13–14) The Ant said __________________________________

____.

9. (Line 15) The Grasshopper said _______________________________

____.

10. (Line 18) The Grasshopper wondered __________________________

____.

11. (Lines 23–24) The Grasshopper thought _______________________

____.

12. (Lines 25–26) The Grasshopper said __________________________

____.

PRACTICE 30 ▶ Check your knowledge. (Chapter 14 Review)
Correct the errors.

1. Excuse me. May I ask if how old are you?

2. I wonder did Rashed pick up something for dinner?

3. I'm unsure what does Lawrence do for a living.

4. Fernando said, "the best time for me to meet would be Thursday morning.

5. Eriko said to me was I coming to the graduation party. I say her that I wasn't.

6. I hope so that I will do well on my final exams.

7. I'm not sure if that the price includes the sales tax or not.

8. My mother said to me that, "How many hours did you spend on your homework?"

9. I told my brother, "Are you going to marry Paula?"

10. I'd like to know how do you do that.

11. My parents knew what did Sam and I do.

12. Is a fact that unexpected things happen in everyone's lives.

13. I'm not sure do I want to travel this summer.

14. I wonder when will the new coffee shop open.

15. Do you know if or not the game will start on time?

16. Sara asked can she borrow my phone.

17. Our teacher wants to know did we finish our homework.

18. Could you tell me what time is it?

PRACTICE 31 ▸ Word search puzzle. (Chapter 14).

Circle the words that are the past tense forms of verbs often used to introduce noun clauses in reported speech. There are seven words in the puzzle.

The words may be horizontal, vertical, or diagonal. The first letter of each word is highlighted in green.

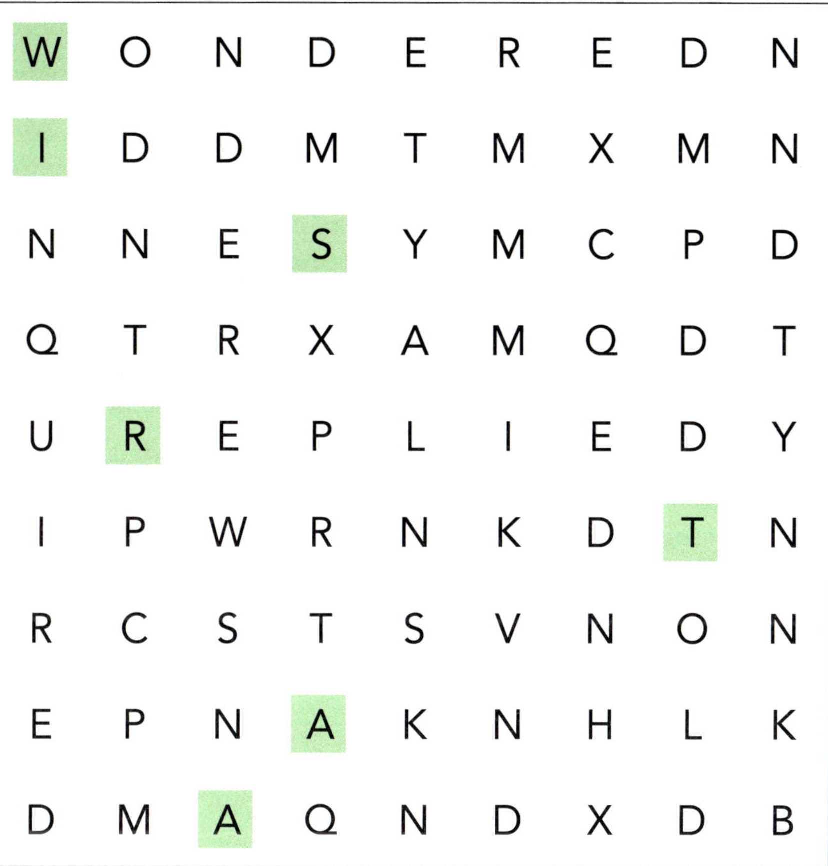

Appendix 1

Phrasal Verbs

PRACTICE 1 ▶ Group A: Phrasal Verbs (separable)
Complete the examples in the chart.

Group A: Phrasal Verbs (separable)		
Verb	**Definition**	**Example**
figure out	find the solution to a problem	I *figured* ___*out*___ the answer.
hand in	give homework, papers, etc., to a teacher	We *handed* __________ our homework.
hand out	give something to this person, then that person, etc.	The teacher *handed* __________ the test papers to the class.
look up	look for information in a dictionary, phone book, online, etc.	I *looked* __________ the store hours online.
make up	invent (a story)	Kids like to *make* __________ stories.
pick up	lift	Tom *picked* __________ the baby.
put down	stop holding or carrying	I *put* __________ the heavy packages.
put off.	postpone	We *put* __________ our trip until next summer.
put on	place clothes on one's body	I *put* __________ my coat before I left.
take off	remove clothes from one's body	I *took* __________ my coat when I arrived.
throw away . . . . . . }	put in the trash, discard	I *threw* __________ my old notebooks.
throw out . . . . }		I *threw* __________ my old notebooks.
turn off	stop a machine or a light	I *turned* __________ the lights and went to bed.
turn on	start a machine or a light	I *turned* __________ the light and read a book.
wake up	stop sleeping	I *woke* __________ at six.
write down	write a note on a piece of paper	I *wrote* his phone number __________.

PRACTICE 2 ▸ Group A.

Complete the sentences with particles from the box.

away	down	in	off	on	out	up

1. Jackson is all wet. I told him to take __________ his clothes and put __________ some dry ones.

2. Lilly made __________ a story. She didn't tell the truth.

3. Alice used her phone to look __________ a word. Then she wrote __________ the definition.

4. Sometimes I postpone doing my homework. I put it __________ till the last minute, but I never hand __________ assignments late.

5. My arms hurt, so I put the baby __________ for a minute. But he started crying right away, so I picked him __________ again.

6. My roommate is messy. He never picks __________ his clothes.

7. I wanted to wake __________ at 7:00, but I didn't get up until 7:30. When the alarm rang, I turned it __________ and went back to sleep.

8. We don't need these receipts anymore. We can throw them __________.

9. When I got my physics test today, I realized that I couldn't figure __________ any of the answers. Our teacher had made a mistake and handed __________ the wrong test!

PRACTICE 3 ▸ Group A.

Choose all the correct completions for each sentence.

1. Akiko turned off   *her phone.*   *the butter.*   *the stove.*
2. I took off   *my coat.*   *my homework.*   *my wedding ring.*
3. Jonas put on   *his shoes.*   *a pencil.*   *the dishes.*
4. Benjamin made up   *a story.*   *a fairy tale.*   *an excuse.*
5. Susanna threw out   *some air.*   *some rotten food.*   *an old shirt.*
6. Antonio put off   *a doctor's appointment.*   *a meeting.*   *a trip.*
7. Max figured out   *a puzzle.*   *a math problem.*   *difficult.*
8. Kyong handed in   *some candy.*   *a report.*   *some late homework.*
9. The secretary wrote down   *a message.*   *a pencil.*   *a phone number.*
10. The mail carrier put down   *a box.*   *the mail truck.*   *a sack of mail.*
11. Mustafa turned off   *the light.*   *the computer.*   *the car engine.*

Complete the examples for the chart.

Group B: Phrasal Verbs (nonseparable)		
Verb	**Definition**	**Example**
call on	ask (someone) to speak in class	The teacher *called* __________ Ali.
come from	originate	Where did these bananas *come* __________ ?
get over	recover from an illness or a shock	Sue *got* __________ her cold quickly.
get off	leave ⎫ a bus/airplane/train/subway	I *got* __________ the bus at First Street.
get on	enter ⎭	I *got* __________ the bus at Fifth Street.
get in/into	enter ⎫ a car, a taxi	I *got* __________ the taxi at the airport.
get out of	leave ⎭	I *got* __________ the taxi at the hotel.
look into	investigate	The police are *looking* __________ the crime.
run into	meet by chance	I *ran* __________ Peter at the store.

Complete the sentences with particles from the list.

> from   in   into   off   on   out of   over

1. When I raised my hand in class, the teacher called __________ me.

2. Josh feels okay today. He got __________ his cold.

3. Last week I flew from Chicago to Miami. I got __________ the plane in Chicago. I got __________ the plane in Miami.

4. Elena took a taxi to the airport. She got __________ the taxi in front of her apartment building. She got __________ the taxi at the airport.

5. I take the bus to school every day. I get __________ the bus at the corner of First Street and Sunset Boulevard. I get __________ the bus just a block away from the classroom building.

6. The receptionist at the power company didn't know why my bill was so high, but she said she would look __________ it.

7. I ran __________ Pierre at the mall. He's married and has ten kids!

8. I ordered some new furniture. It came __________ India.

Complete each sentence in Column A with the correct phrase from Column B.

Example: Annette speaks both French and English because she comes . . .

> *Annette speaks both French and English because she comes from Quebec.*

Column A	Column B
1. Annette speaks both French and English because she comes	a. into your request for medical records.
2. When Sylvia lost her job, it took her several weeks to get	✓b. from Quebec.

3. Our office will need several days to look	c. over the shock.
4. When a plane lands, the first-class passengers get	d. into a taxi and went to the airport.
5. While I was walking in the mall, I ran	e. on unprepared students.
6. When he left the hotel, David got	f. into several friends from high school.
7. Mrs. Riley, our math teacher, often calls	g. off first.

PRACTICE 7 ▸ Group C.

Complete the examples for the chart.

Group C: Phrasal Verbs (separable)		
Verb	**Definition**	**Example**
ask out.	ask (someone) to go on a date	Tom *asked* Emily ___________. They went to a movie.
call back	return a telephone call	I'll *call* you ___________ tomorrow.
call off	cancel	We *called* ___________ the picnic because of the rain.
call up	make a telephone call	I *called* ___________ my friend in New York.
give back	return something to someone	I borrowed Lee's pen, then I *gave* it ___________.
hang up	hang on a hanger or a hook	I *hung* my coat ___________ in the closet.
pay back	return borrowed money to someone	Thanks for the loan. I'll *pay* you ___________ soon.
put away	put something in its usual or proper place	I *put* the clean dishes ___________.
put back	return something to its original place	I *put* my books ___________ into my bag.
put out.	extinguish (stop) a fire, a cigarette	We *put* ___________ the campfire before we left.
shut off	stop a machine or light, turn off	I *shut* ___________ the copy machine before I left the office.
try on.	put on clothing to see if it fits	I *tried* ___________ several pairs of shoes.
turn down	decrease the volume	Chris *turned* ___________ the music. It was too loud.
turn up	increase the volume	Michael *turned* ___________ the music. He likes loud music.

Complete the sentences with particles from the box.

away	back	down	off	on	out	up

1. You still owe me the money I lent you. When are you going to pay me __________?

2. Turn __________ the music! It's too loud! I can't hear myself think.

3. Debra put __________ the fire in the oven with a fire extinguisher.

4. I'll wash and dry the dishes, and you can put them __________ in the cabinet.

5. Before you buy shoes, you should try them __________ to see if they fit.

6. I can't hear the news. Could you please turn __________ the TV?

7. You can borrow my stapler, but please give it __________ to me before you leave the office.

8. I didn't hear anyone on the other end of the phone, so I hung __________.

9. You can look at these books, but please put them __________ on the shelf when you're finished.

10. Bob hasn't paid his electric bill for months, so the electric company shut his power __________.

11. A: I hear that Tom asked you __________ for next Saturday night.

   B: Yes, he did. He called me __________ a couple of hours ago and invited me to a soccer game.

   A: The game has been called __________ because it's raining. Didn't you hear about it?

   B: No, I didn't. I'd better call Tom __________ and ask him what he wants to do instead.

PRACTICE 9 ▸ Phrasal verbs: separable. (Groups A, B, C)

Complete the sentences with a given particle where possible. If not possible, write "X."

1. *out*	a. Paulo asked ___*out*___ one of his classmates.
	b. Paulo asked one of his classmates ___*out*___.
2. *on*	a. The teacher called ___*on*___ Ted for the answer.
	b. The teacher called Ted ___*X*___ for the answer.
3. *into*	a. The police are looking __________ the crime, but they need help from the public to solve it.
	b. The police are looking the crime __________, but they need help from the public to solve it.
4. *into*	a. Khalifa ran his cousin __________ at the store.
	b. Khalifa ran __________ his cousin at the store.
5. *up*	a. Claire turned __________ the ringer on her phone.
	b. Claire turned the ringer on her phone __________.
6. *away*	a. Dr. Benson threw __________ a valuable coin by mistake.
	b. Dr. Benson threw a valuable coin __________ by mistake.
7. *down*	a. Yumi's baby cries whenever she puts him __________.
	b. Yumi's baby cries whenever she puts __________ him.
8. *up*	a. Would you please wake __________ me in one hour?
	b. Would you please wake me __________ in one hour?

9. *away*	a. You can leave the dishes. I'll put them __________ later.
	b. You can leave the dishes. I'll put __________ them later.
10. *up*	a. When Joan feels lonely, she calls __________ a friend and talks for a while.
	b. When Joan feels lonely, she calls a friend __________ and talks for a while.
11. *off*	a. The hill was so steep that I had to get __________ my bicycle and walk.
	b. The hill was so steep that I had to get my bicycle __________ and walk.
12. *from*	a. This fruit is very fresh. It came __________ my garden.
	b. This fruit is very fresh. It came my garden __________.

PRACTICE 10 ▸ Group D.

Complete the examples.

Group D: Phrasal Verbs (separable)		
Verb	**Definition**	**Example**
cross out	draw a line through	I *crossed* __________ the misspelled word.
fill in	complete by writing in a blank space	We *fill* __________ the blanks in grammar exercises.
fill out	write information on a form	I *filled* __________ a job application.
fill up	fill completely with gas, water, coffee, etc.	We *filled* __________ the gas tank.
find out	discover information	I *found* __________ where he lives.
have on	wear	She *has* a blue blouse __________.
look over	examine carefully	*Look* __________ your paper for errors before you hand it in.
point out	call attention to	The teacher *pointed* __________ a misspelling.
print out	create a paper copy	Would you like me to *print* __________ your receipt, or should I email you a copy?
tear down	destroy a building	They *tore* __________ the old house and built a new one.
tear out (of)	remove (paper) by tearing	I *tore* a sheet of paper __________ __________ my notebook.
tear up	tear into small pieces	I *tore* __________ the documents with my credit card information.
turn around . . . . . } **turn back** . . . . }	change to the opposite direction	After a mile, we *turned* __________ / __________.
turn over	turn the top side to the bottom	I *turned* the paper __________ and wrote on the back.

Complete the sentences with particles from the box.

around	back	down	in	of	out	over	up

1. You're going to burn those pancakes! You need to turn them _____*over*_____ and cook the other side.

2. When the teacher finds a mistake in our writing, she points it __________ so we can correct it.

3. When I write words in this practice, I am filling __________ the blanks.

4. When I discover new information, I find something __________.

5. When I finish writing my essay, I will print it __________.

6. When buildings are old and dangerous, we tear them __________.

7. When I turn and go in the opposite direction, I turn __________.

8. When I remove a piece of paper from a spiral notebook, I tear the paper __________ my notebook.

9. When I write something that I don't want anybody else to see, I tear the paper into tiny pieces. I tear __________ the paper.

10. When I write information on an application form, I fill the form __________.

11. When I make a mistake in something I write, I erase the mistake if I'm using a pencil. If I'm using a pen, I cross the mistake __________ by drawing a line through it.

12. When my juice glass is empty, I fill it __________ again if I'm still thirsty.

13. When I check my homework carefully before I give it to the teacher, I look it __________.

PRACTICE 12 ▶ Groups A, B, C, D

Complete the sentences with the particles in *italics*. The particles may be used more than once or not at all.

1. *out, away, back, down, off, on*

   Sofie . . .

   a. put _____*off*_____ her vacation because she was sick.

   b. put __________ her boots to go out in the rain.

   c. put the phone __________ when she saw a spider crawling toward her.

   d. put her things __________ in her suitcase after the customs officer checked them.

   e. put __________ the stovetop fire with a small fire extinguisher.

   f. put __________ all the groceries she bought before she started dinner.

2. *out, in, up*

   James . . .

   a. handed __________ his financial report before the due date.

   b. handed __________ thank-you gifts to his staff for their hard work.

3. *into, off, on, up, over, out of*

Leah . . .

   a. got __________ the flu in three days and felt wonderful.

   b. got __________ the bus and walked home.

   c. got __________ the bus and sat down behind the driver.

   d. got __________ a taxi and buckled her seatbelt.

   e. paid the driver and got __________ the taxi.

4. *in, down, up, out*

   a. This book has a few pages missing. The baby tore them __________.

   b. Before I throw my credit card receipts away, I tear them __________. I don't want anyone to read them.

   c. The building across the street will be torn __________ to make room for a parking garage.

5. *over, into, up*

   a. The neighbors asked the sheriff to look __________ a crime in their neighborhood.

   b. The sheriff looked __________ a suspect's address on the computer.

   c. The sheriff took the suspect's ID, looked it __________ slowly, and decided it was fake.

6. *off, down, up, back*

   a. I called Chloe __________ several times but got no answer. I'm a little worried.

   b. The meeting was called __________ because the chairperson was sick.

   c. Jack called and left a message. I'll call him __________ after dinner.

7. *over, up, in, off, back*

   a. I'm trying to do homework, but your music is very loud. It's hard to concentrate. Please turn it __________.

   b. It's cold, and I'm tired. Let's turn __________ and go home.

   c. Could I turn __________ the TV? I can't hear it very well.

   d. Joe, the meat needs to be cooked on the other side. Would you turn it __________, please?

8. *in, out, up*

   a. I forgot to fill __________ a couple of blanks on the test. I hope I passed.

   b. Can I take this application home and fill it __________? I don't have much time now.

   c. Jack carries a thermos bottle to work. He fills __________ his cup when he gets thirsty.

   d. Gas is expensive. It costs a lot to fill __________ my tank.

Complete the examples for the chart.

Group E: Phrasal Verbs (separable)		
Verb	**Definition**	**Example**
blow out	extinguish (a match, a candle)	He *blew* the candles __________ .
bring back	return	She *brought* my books __________ to me.
bring up	(1) raise (children)	The Lees *brought* __________ six children.
	(2) mention, start to talk about	He *brought* the news __________ in conversation.
cheer up	make happier	The good news *cheered* me __________ .
clean up	make neat and clean	I *cleaned* __________ my apartment.
give away	donate, get rid of by giving	I didn't sell my old bike. I *gave* it __________ .
help out	assist (someone)	Could you please *help* me __________ ?
lay off	stop employment	The company *laid* __________ 100 workers.
leave on	(1) not turn off (a light, a machine)	Please *leave* the light __________ . I can't see.
	(2) not take off (clothing)	I *left* my coat __________ during class.
take back	return	She *took* a book __________ to the library.
take out	invite out and pay for	He *took* Mary __________ . They went to a movie.
talk over	discuss	We *talked* the problem __________ .
think over	consider	I *thought* the problem __________ .
work out	solve	We *worked* the problem __________ .

Complete the sentences with particles from the box.

> away   back   off   on   out   over   up

1. It's pretty chilly in here. You might want to leave your jacket __________ .

2. My father speaks with an Australian accent. He was brought __________ in Australia.

3. The Smiths have marriage problems, but they are trying to work them __________ . They talk them __________ as soon as they occur.

4. Isabel blew __________ the candles on her birthday cake.

5. My roommate gives __________ his old clothes to homeless people. He tries to help them __________ as often as possible.

6. I took my parents __________ to a restaurant for their anniversary. Then I cleaned __________ their house the next day for them.

7. These are bad economic times. Businesses are laying __________ hundreds of workers.

8. The store's return policy is that you can bring clothes __________ within two weeks if you have a receipt.

9. I'm meeting with my supervisor later today. I'm going to bring __________ the idea of a raise.

10. I won't be home until midnight, so please leave some lights __________ .

11. When I'm sad, my friends try to cheer me __________ .

12. Are you sure you want to change jobs? Do you want to think it __________ some more?

13. I hate to bring this problem __________, but we need to talk about it.

14. I can't sell this old table. I guess I'll give it __________. Someone will be able to use it.

15. My parents usually help me __________ when I'm having trouble paying my bills.

16. You can borrow my tools, but when you finish, be sure to put them __________.

PRACTICE 15 ▸ Group F.

Complete the examples for the chart.

Group F: Phrasal Verbs (intransitive)		
Verb	**Definition**	**Example**
break down	stop functioning properly	My car *broke* __________ on the highway.
break out	happen suddenly	War *broke* __________ between the two countries.
break up	separate, end a relationship	Ann and Tom *broke* __________.
come in	enter a room or building	May I *come* __________?
dress up	put on nice clothes	People usually *dress* __________ for weddings.
eat out	eat outside of one's home	Would you like to *eat* __________ tonight?
fall down	fall to the ground	I *fell* __________ and hurt myself.
get up	get out of bed in the morning	What time did you *get* __________ this morning?
give up	quit doing something or quit trying	I can't do it. I *give* __________.
go on	continue	Let's not stop. Let's *go* __________.
go out	not stay home	Jane *went* __________ with her friends last night.
hang up	end a telephone conversation	When we finished talking, I *hung* __________.
move in (to)	start living in a new home	Some people *moved* __________ next door to me.
move out (of)	stop living at a place	My roommate is *moving* __________.
show up	come, appear	Jack *showed* __________ late for the meeting.
sit back	put one's back against a chair back	*Sit* __________ and relax. I'll get you a drink.
sit down	go from standing to sitting	Please *sit* __________.
speak up	(1) speak louder I can't hear you.	You'll have to *speak* __________.
	(2) express one's opinion without fear	
stand up	go from sitting to standing	I *stood* __________ and walked to the door.
start over	begin again	I lost count, so I *started* __________.
stay up	not go to bed	I *stayed* __________ late last night.
take off	ascend in an airplane	The plane *took* __________ 30 minutes late.

Complete the sentences with particles from the box.

back	down	in	off	on	out	over	up

1. The plane shook a little when it took __________. It made me nervous.

2. I'm afraid we can't hear you in the back of the room. Could you please speak __________?

3. My chemistry teacher is so confusing. I can't understand a thing! I think I'll just drop the class and start __________ with a new teacher next term.

4. I was late to work. The bus broke __________, and we had to wait for another.

5. Mrs. Taylor is in the hospital again. She fell __________ and broke her hip.

6. Jim and Sarah aren't getting married. They had a fight and broke __________ last night.

7. Julian's at the doctor's office. He broke __________ in a rash last night, and he doesn't know what it is.

8. I'm very nervous when I fly. I can't just sit __________ and relax.

9. Sometimes when I stand __________ too fast, I get dizzy.

10. Someone keeps calling and hanging __________. It's very annoying.

11. Sorry, I didn't mean to interrupt you. Please go __________.

12. A: Professor Wilson, do you have a minute?

    B: Sure. Come __________ and sit __________.

PRACTICE 17 ▸ Group F.

Complete the sentences with particles from the box.

into	of	out	up

1. *Leo is lazy and irresponsible. He . . .*

   a. broke _____*up*_____ with his girlfriend because she didn't want to wash his clothes.

   b. stayed __________ all night and didn't come home until morning.

   c. showed __________ late for class without his homework.

   d. goes __________ with friends to parties on school nights.

   e. eats __________ at restaurants every day because he doesn't like to cook.

   f. moved __________ __________ his apartment without telling the manager.

2. *Amy is careful and responsible. She . . .*

   a. goes to bed very early. She never stays __________ past 9:00.

   b. gets __________ at 5:00 every morning.

   c. speaks __________ in class when no one will answer.

   d. dresses __________ for school.

   e. moved __________ an apartment close to her school.

   f. never gives __________ when she gets frustrated.

Complete the examples for the chart.

Group G: Phrasal Verbs (three-word)		
Verb	**Definition**	**Example**
drop in (on)	visit without calling first or without an invitation	We *dropped* _________ _________ my aunt.
drop out (of)	stop attending (school)	Beth *dropped* _________ _________ graduate school.
get along (with)	have a good relationship with	I *get* _________ well _________ my roommate.
get back (from)	return from (a trip)	When did you *get* _________ _________ Hawaii?
get through (with)	finish	I *got* _________ _________ my work before noon.
grow up (in)	become an adult	Anika *grew* _________ _________ Sweden.
look out (for)	be careful	*Look* _________ _________ that car!
run out (of)	finish the supply of (something)	We *ran* _________ _________ gas.
sign up (for)	put one's own name on a list	Did you *sign* _________ _________ the school trip?
watch out (for)	be careful	*Watch* _________ _________ that car!

Complete the phrasal verbs.

1. Look _________! There's a car coming! Look _________ _________ the truck too!

2. I grew up in New Zealand. Where did you grow _________?

3. If you want to be in the class, you have to sign _________ _________ it first.

4. I couldn't finish the examination. I ran _________ _________ time.

5. Joe is really tired. He just got _________ _________ a 10-day mountain climbing trip.

6. Jack dropped _________ _________ school last week. His parents are upset.

7. Watch _________ _________ the truck! It has a loose wheel.

8. Joanne got _________ _________ her work early, so she's leaving for vacation today.

9. My neighbor likes to drop _________ _________ us during dinner. I think she's lonely.

10. A: I want to move to another dorm room.

    B: Why?

    A: I don't get _________ _________ my roommate. She's messy and plays loud music when I'm trying to study.

Complete each sentence with the correct word from the box.

assignment	✓dance class	Mexico	paint
rocks	snakes	the hospital	their neighbors

1. Martin signed up for a _dance class_. It starts next week.

2. The Hansens get along well with __________. They even take vacations together.

3. I can't finish the living room walls because I've run out of __________.

4. The highway sign said to watch out for __________. They roll down the hills and sometimes hit cars.

5. As soon as I get through with this __________, we can go to lunch. I have just one more problem to figure out.

6. Naomi speaks Spanish because she grew up in __________.

7. Let's go check on Hannah. She just got back from __________.

8. Look out for __________ on the path. They're not poisonous, but they might startle you.

PRACTICE 21 ▶ Group H.

Complete the examples.

Group H: Phrasal Verbs (three-word)		
Verb	**Definition**	**Example**
come along (with)	accompany	Do you want to *come* __________ __________ us?
come over (to)	visit the speaker's place	Some friends are *coming* __________ tonight.
cut out (of)	remove	I *cut* sugar __________ __________ my diet.
find out (about)	discover information about	When did you *find* __________ __________ the problem?
get together (with)	join, meet	Let's *get* __________ after work today.
go back (to)	return to a place	I *went* __________ __________ work after my illness.
go over (to)	(1) approach	I *went* __________ __________ the window.
	(2) visit another's home	Let's *go* __________ __________ Jim's tonight.
hang around (with)		John likes to *hang* __________ the coffee shop.
hang out (with)	spend time relaxing	Kids like to *hang* __________ __________ each other.
keep away (from)	not give to	*Keep* sharp knives __________ __________ children.
set out (for)	begin a trip	We *set* __________ __________ the mountain at sunrise.
sit around (with)	sit and do nothing	Don't *sit* __________ all day. Do something!

Complete each sentence with two particles.

1. Before we consider buying a home in this area, we'd like to find ___*out*___ more ___*about*___ the schools.

2. The mountain climbers set __________ __________ the summit at dawn and reached it by lunchtime.

3. When my grandma was 65, she decided to go __________ __________ school and get a college degree.

4. Teenagers like to hang __________ __________ friends after school.

5. Susie needs to keep __________ __________ the dog. She's allergic to the fur.

6. I'm going shopping. Do you want to come __________ __________ me?

7. I invited my class to come __________ __________ our beach house on Saturday.

8. I'm too busy these days. I need to cut something __________ __________ my schedule.

9. A: Did you go __________ __________ Brian's last night?

   B: No, he wasn't home, so I just sat __________ my apartment __________ my cat.

PRACTICE 23 ▶ Group H.

Complete the sentences with particles that will give the same meanings as the <u>underlined</u> words.

1. I'd like to <u>get information</u> about the company. I want to find ___*out*___ ___*about*___ it before I apply for a job there.

2. The two brothers <u>began their</u> fishing <u>trip</u> to the lake before sunrise. They set __________ early because they wanted to be the first ones there.

3. What time is the supervisor <u>returning</u>? I'd like to talk to him when he gets __________ .

4. Mark won't be home for dinner. He plans to <u>join</u> his co-workers for a party. They only get __________ once a year, so Mark is looking forward to it.

5. The dog was growling when the dog catcher <u>approached</u> him. The dog catcher went __________ __________ him very carefully.

Appendix 2
Preposition Combinations

PRACTICE 1 ▸ Group A.*

Test yourself and practice the preposition combinations. Follow these steps:

(1) Cover the ANSWERS column with a piece of paper.

(2) Complete the SENTENCES.

(3) Then remove the paper and check your answers.

(4) Then cover both the ANSWERS and the SENTENCES to complete your own REFERENCE LIST.

(5) Again check your answers.

	Preposition Combinations: Group A	
Answers	**Sentences**	**Reference List**
from	He was absent ___*from*___ work.	**be absent** ___*from*___ s.t.**
of	I'm afraid ___*of*___ rats.	**be afraid** ___*of*___ s.t./s.o.**
about	I'm angry ___*about*___ it.	**be angry** _____________ s.t.
at / with	I'm angry _____________ you.	**be angry** _____________ s.o.
about	I'm curious_____________ many things.	**be curious** _____________ s.t./s.o.
to	This is equal _____________ that.	**be equal** _____________ s.t./s.o.
with	I'm familiar _____________ that book.	**be familiar** _____________ s.t./s.o.
of	The room is full _____________ people.	**be full** _____________ (*people/things*)
for	I'm happy _____________ you.	**be happy** _____________ s.o.
about	I'm happy _____________ your good luck	**be happy** _____________ s.t.
to	He's kind _____________ people and animals.	**be kind** _____________ s.o.
to	She's always nice _____________ me.	**be nice** _____________ s.o.
to	Are you polite _____________ strangers?	**be polite** _____________ s.o.
for	I'm ready _____________ my trip.	**be ready** _____________ s.t.
for	She's thirsty _____________ lemonade.	**be thirsty** _____________ s.t.

**s.t. = "something"; s.o. = "someone"

Match each phrase in Column A with a phrase in Column B. Use each phrase only once.

Column A	Column B
1. Our dog is afraid _____b_____ .	a. about his team's win
2. The class is curious _____ .	✓b. of cats
3. Mr. White is angry _____ .	c. for a glass of water
4. Several nurses have been absent _____ .	d. for the start of school
5. After gardening all day, Hannah was thirsty _____ .	e. from work due to illness
6. The workers are angry _____ .	f. about the snake in the cage
7. The baseball coach was happy _____ .	g. to everyone
8. The kitchen cupboard is full _____ .	h. of canned foods
9. I'm not ready _____ .	i. about their low pay
10. It's important to be kind _____ .	j. at his dog for chewing his shoes

PRACTICE 3 ▶ Group A.

Complete the sentences with prepositions.

1. Mr. Porter is nice __________ everyone.

2. One inch is equal __________ 2.54 centimeters.

3. Joe has good manners. He's always polite __________ everyone.

4. I'm not familiar __________ that book. Who wrote it?

5. Anna got a good job that pays well. I'm very happy __________ her.

6. Anna is very happy __________ getting a new job.

7. My backpack is full __________ books.

8. The workers were angry __________ the decrease in their pay.

9. Half the students were absent __________ class yesterday. There is a flu virus going around.

10. I'm not familiar __________ that movie. Who is in it?

11. Kids ask a lot of questions. They are curious __________ everything.

12. William has been afraid __________ spiders since he was a kid.

PRACTICE 4 ▶ Group B.

The prepositions in the column on the left are the correct completions for the blanks. Follow the same steps you used for Group A on page 254.

Preposition Combinations: Group B		
Answers	**Sentences**	**Reference List**
for	I admire you __________ your honesty.	**admire** s.o. __________ s.t.
for	He applied __________ a job.	**apply** __________ s.t.
with	I argued __________ my husband.	**argue** __________ s.o.

about / over	We argued _____________ money.	**argue** _____________ s.t.
in	My parents believe _____________ me.	**believe** _____________ s.o./s.t.
from	I borrowed a book _____________ Oscar.	**borrow** s.t. _____________ s.o.
with	I discussed the problem _____________ Jane.	**discuss** s.t. _____________ s.o.
with	Please help me _____________ this.	**help** s.o. _____________ s.t.
to	I introduced Sam _____________ Mackenzie.	**introduce** s.o. _____________ s.o./s.t.
at	I laughed _____________ the joke.	**laugh** _____________ s.o./s.t.
for	I'm leaving _____________ Rome next week.	**leave** _____________ (*a place*)
at	Don't stare _____________ me.	**stare** _____________ s.o./s.t.

PRACTICE 5 ▸ Group B.

Complete the sentences with prepositions.

1. I borrowed this phone charger __________ Pedro.

2. Could you please help me __________ these heavy bags?

3. Emma, I'd like to introduce you __________ Andrew Kennedy.

4. You shouldn't stare __________ people. It's not polite.

5. Do you believe __________ ghosts?

6. Are you laughing __________ my mistake?

7. I admire my father __________ his honesty and intelligence.

8. I argued __________ Elena __________ politics.

9. I discussed my educational plans __________ my parents.

10. I applied __________ admission to the university.

11. We're leaving __________ Cairo next week.

PRACTICE 6 ▸ Groups A and B.

Complete the sentences with prepositions.

1. Daniel is always nice __________ everyone.

2. A: How long do you need to keep the Spanish book you borrowed __________ me?

   B: I'd like to keep it until I'm ready __________ the exam next week.

3. A: Why weren't you more polite __________ Alan's friend?

   B: Because he kept staring __________ me all evening. He made me nervous.

4. $^5/_{10}$ is equal __________ ½.

5. You did a lot of shopping. The refrigerator is full __________ food.

6. Where is the nearest coffee shop? I'm thirsty __________ an iced coffee.

7. I need to discuss my grade __________ my professor.

8. There's a new position for a project manager at my company. You should apply __________ it.

The prepositions in the column on the left are the correct completions for the blanks. Follow the same steps you used for Group A on page 254.

Answers	Sentences	Reference List
of	I'm aware ___________ the problem.	**be aware** ___________ s.o./s.t.
for	Smoking is bad ___________ you.	**be bad** ___________ s.o./s.t.
to	The solution is clear ___________ me.	**be clear** ___________ s.o
about	Alex is crazy ___________ football.	**be crazy** ___________ s.t.
from	Jane is very different ___________ me.	**be different** ___________ s.o./s.t.
for	Venice is famous ___________ its canals.	**be famous** ___________ s.t.
to / with	She's friendly ___________ everyone.	**be friendly** ___________ s.o.
for	Fresh fruit is good ___________ you.	**be good** ___________ s.o.
for	I'm hungry ___________ some chocolate.	**be hungry** ___________ s.t.
in	I'm interested ___________ art.	**be interested** ___________ s.t.
about	I'm nervous ___________ my test scores.	**be nervous** ___________ s.t.
with	I'm patient ___________ children.	**be patient** ___________ s.o.
of	My parents are proud ___________ me.	**be proud** ___________ s.o./s.t.
for	Who's responsible ___________ this?	**be responsible** ___________ s.o./s.t.
about	I'm sad ___________ losing my job.	**be sad** ___________ s.t.
to	A lemon is similar ___________ a lime.	**be similar** ___________ s.o./s.t.
of / about	I'm sure ___________ the facts.	**be sure** ___________ s.t.

PRACTICE 8 ▸ Group C.

Complete the sentences with prepositions.

1. I don't understand that sentence. It isn't clear _________ me.
2. Mark Twain is famous _________ his novels about life on the Mississippi River.
3. Are you hungry _________ for lunch yet?
4. Our daughter graduated from college. We're very proud _________ her.
5. Sugar isn't good _________ you. It is bad _________ your teeth.
6. Who was responsible _________ the accident?
7. My coat is similar _________ yours but different _________ Ben's.
8. Some people aren't friendly _________ strangers.
9. My daughter is crazy _________ horses. She is very interested _________ them.
10. Sara knows what she's talking about. She's sure _________ her facts.

Complete the sentences with prepositions.

1. Dr. Nelson, a heart specialist, is . . .

   a. proud _________ her work.

   b. famous _________ her medical expertise.

   c. sure _________ her skills.

   d. familiar _________ the latest techniques.

   e. patient _________ her patients.

   f. aware _________ the stresses of her job.

   g. interested _________ her patients' lives.

   h. kind _________ her patients' families.

2. Her patient, Ms. Green, is . . .

   a. sad _________ her illness.

   b. nervous _________ an upcoming surgery.

   c. aware _________ the risks of surgery.

   d. full _________ hope.

   e. curious _________ alternative medicine.

   f. ready _________ a quick recovery.

PRACTICE 10 ▸ Group D.

The prepositions in the column on the left are the correct completions for the blanks. Follow the same steps you used for Group A on page 254.

	Preposition Combinations: Group D	
Answers	**Sentences**	**Reference List**
with	I agree _________ you.	**agree** _________ s.o.
about	I agree with you _________ that.	**agree with** s.o. _________ s.t.
in	We arrived _________ Toronto at six.	**arrive** _________ (*a city/country*)
at	We arrived _________ the hotel.	**arrive** _________ (*a building/room*)
about	We all complain _________ the weather.	**complain** _________ s.o./s.t.
of	A book consists _________ printed pages.	**consist** _________ s.t.
with	I disagree _________ you.	**disagree** _________ s.o.
about	I disagree with you _________ that.	**disagree with** s.o. _________ s.t.
from	She graduated _________ Reed College.	**graduate** _________ (*a place*)
to	Luke invited me _________ the game.	**invite** s.o. _________ s.t.
to	We listened _________ some music.	**listen** _________ s.o./s.t.
for	Jack paid _________ my dinner.	**pay** _________ s.t.
to	I talked _________ Annie on the phone.	**talk** _________ s.o.

about	We talked _____________ her problem.	**talk** _____________ s.t.
on	A salesman waited _____________ a customer.	**wait** _____________ s.o.
for	We waited _____________ the bus.	**wait** _____________ s.t.
about	Olivia complained to me _____________ my dog.	**complain to** s.o. _____________ s.t.

PRACTICE 11 ▸ Group D.

Complete the sentences with prepositions.

1. Zachary paid _________ his airplane ticket in cash.

2. Natalie graduated _________ high school two years ago.

3. I waited _________ the bus.

4. Jim is a waiter. He waits _________ customers at a restaurant.

5. I have a different opinion. I don't agree _________ you.

6. I arrived _________ this city last month.

7. I arrived _________ the airport around eight.

8. I listened _________ the news on TV last night.

9. The supervisor agreed _________ the employees' decision to work longer days and shorter weeks.

10. This practice consists _________ verbs that are followed by certain prepositions.

11. Adrian invited me _________ his party.

12. I complained _________ the building manager_________ the leaky faucet in the kitchen.

13. Megan disagreed _________ her father _________ the amount of her weekly allowance.

14. Did you talk _________ Professor Adams _________ your grades?

PRACTICE 12 ▸ Groups A, B, and D.

Complete the sentences with prepositions.

1. Everyone is talking _________ the explosion in the high school chemistry lab.

2. Carlos was absent _________ class six times last term.

3. Fruit consists mostly _________ water.

4. Our children are very polite _________ adults.

5. Three centimeters is equal _________ approximately one and a half inches.

6. I borrowed some clothes _________ my best friend.

7. Are you familiar _________ ancient Greek history?

8. I discussed my problem _________ my uncle.

9. I admire you _________ your ability to laugh _________ yourself when you make a silly mistake.

10. A: Are you two arguing _________ each other _________ money again?

    B: Yeah, listen _________ this.

    A: Shhh. I don't want to hear any of this. Stop complaining _________ me _________ your finances.
    I don't agree with either of you.

PRACTICE 13 ▶ Group E.

The prepositions in the column on the left are the correct completions for the blanks. Follow the same steps you used for Group A on page 254.

	Preposition Combinations: Group E	
Answers	Sentences	Reference List
about	She asked me ___________ my trip.	**ask** s.o. ___________ s.t. (inquire)
for	She asked me ___________ my advice.	**ask** s.o. ___________ s.t. (request)
to	This book belongs ___________ me.	**belong** ___________ s.o.
about / of	I dreamed ___________ going to Paris.	**dream** ___________ s.o./s.t.
about	Do you know anything ___________ jazz?	**know** ___________ s.t.
at	I'm looking ___________ this page.	**look** ___________ s.o./s.t.
for	I'm looking ___________ my lost keys.	**look** ___________ s.o./s.t. (search)
like	Anna looks ___________ her sister.	**look** ___________ s.o. (resemble)
to	I'm looking forward ___________ vacation.	**look forward** ___________ s.t.
to	Your opinion doesn't matter ___________ me.	**matter** ___________ s.o.
with	Something is the matter ___________ the cat.	**be the matter** ___________ s.o./s.t.
for	I'm searching ___________ my lost keys.	**search** ___________ s.o./s.t.
from	She separated the boys ___________ the girls.	**separate** (*this*) ___________ (*that*)
about / of	I warned them ___________ the danger.	**warn** s.o. ___________ s.t.

PRACTICE 14 ▶ Group E.

Complete the sentences with prepositions.

1. What's the matter _________ Charlie? Is he hurt?

2. We can go out for dinner, or we can eat at home. It doesn't matter _________ me.

3. To make this recipe, you have to separate the egg whites _________ the yolks.

4. I don't know anything _________ astrology.

5. I'm looking forward _________ my vacation next month.

6. Isabel dreamed _________ dancing last night.

7. Right now I'm doing homework. I'm looking _________ my book.

8. Jim can't find his book. He's looking _________ it.

9. Jim is searching _________ his book.

10. I asked the waitress _________ another cup of coffee.

11. I asked Rebecca _________ her trip to Japan.

12. Does this pen belong _________ you?

13. The city was warned _________ the hurricane in advance.

14. Do you think Jon looks _________ his father or his mother?

15. Magda is always looking _________ her keys. She seems pretty disorganized.

16. Look _________ those clouds. It's going to rain.

Make sentences by matching each phrase in Column A with a phrase in Column B. Use each phrase only once.

Column A	Column B
1. The police are searching ______ .	a. about monsters and dragons
2. The baby keeps looking ______ .	b. to their 20th wedding anniversary
3. Once again, Julie is looking ______ .	c. for her glasses. She always misplaces them
4. In this picture, Paula looks ______ .	d. about the schools in this area
5. The Browns are looking forward ______ .	e. about high winds on the bridge
6. Before you do the wash, you need to separate the darks ______ .	f. with this car. It's making strange noises
7. Sometimes Joey is afraid to sleep. He often dreams ______ .	g. for the suspect
8. Something's the matter ______ .	h. from the whites
9. The sign on the highway warned drivers ______ .	i. at the TV screen. It has bright colors
10. We're planning to move here. Do you know much ______ ?	j. like her mother. The resemblance is very strong

PRACTICE 16 ▶ Group F.

The prepositions in the column on the left are the correct completions for the blanks. Follow the same steps you used for Group A on page 254.

Answers	Sentences	Reference List
to	I apologized ______________ my friend.	**apologize** ______________ s.o.
for	I apologized ______________ my behavior.	**apologize** ______________ s.t.
of	I don't approve ______________ Scott's behavior.	**approve** ______________ s.t.
to / with	I compared this book ______________ that book.	**compare** (*this*) ______________ (*that*)*
on	I depend ______________ my family.	**depend** ______________ s.o./s.t.
of / from	He died ______________ heart disease.	**die** ______________ s.t.
from	The teacher excused me ______________ class.	**excuse** s.o. ______________ s.t.
for	I excused him ______________ his mistake.	**excuse** s.o. ______________ s.t. (forgive)
for	I forgave him ______________ his mistake.	**forgive** s.o. ______________ s.t.
of	I got rid ______________ my old clothes.	**get rid** ______________ s.o./s.t.
to	What happened ______________ your car?	**happen** ______________ s.o./s.t.
on	I insist ______________ the truth.	**insist** ______________ s.t.
from	I protected my eyes ______________ the sun.	**protect** s.o./s.t. ______________ s.o./s.t.
on	I am relying ______________ you to help me.	**rely** ______________ s.o./s.t.
of	Mr. Lee took care ______________ the problem.	**take care** ______________ s.o./s.t.
for	Thank you ______________ your help.	**thank** s.o. ______________ s.t.

*Also possible: *I compared this and that.* (*And* is not a preposition. A parallel structure with *and* may follow *compare.*)

Complete the sentences with prepositions.

1. I apologized __________ Ann __________ stepping on her toe.

2. I thanked Sam __________ helping me fix my car.

3. My grandfather doesn't approve __________ gambling.

4. Please forgive me __________ forgetting your birthday.

5. My friend insisted __________ taking me to the airport.

6. Please excuse me __________ being late.

7. Children depend __________ their parents for love and support.

8. In my composition, I compared this city __________ my hometown.

9. Umbrellas protect people __________ rain.

10. We're relying __________ Jason to help us move into our new apartment.

11. We had mice in the house, so we set some traps to get rid __________ them.

12. Who is taking care __________ the children while you are gone?

13. What happened __________ your finger? Did you cut it?

14. My manager excused me __________ the meeting when I became ill.

15. What did Mr. Hill die __________?

Write "C" beside the correct sentences. Write "I" beside those that are incorrect. In some cases, both may be correct.

1. a. ____C____ I need to be excused from class tomorrow.

   b. ____C____ My professor excused me for being late.

2. a. ____C____ Do you approve of your government's international policies?

   b. ____I____ Do you approve on the new seatbelt law?

3. a. __________ I apologized for the car accident.

   b. __________ I apologized to Mary's parents.

4. a. __________ Why did you get rid over your truck? It was in great condition.

   b. __________ I got rid of several boxes of old magazines.

5. a. __________ Pierre died of a heart attack.

   b. __________ Pierre's father also died from heart problems.

6. a. __________ It's not a good idea to compare one student to another.

   b. __________ I wish my parents wouldn't compare me with my brother.

7. a. __________ We can rely on Lesley to keep a secret.

   b. __________ There are several people whom my elderly parents rely in for assistance.

8. a. __________ You can relax. I took care about your problem.

   b. __________ The nurses take wonderful care of their patients at Valley Hospital.

The prepositions in the column on the left are the correct completions for the blanks. Follow the same steps you used for Group A on page 254.

Answers	Sentences	Reference List
to	I'm accustomed _____________ hot weather.	**be accustomed** _____________ s.t.
to	I added a name _____________ my address book.	**add** (*this*) _____________ (*that*)
on	I'm concentrating _____________ the lecture.	**concentrate** _____________ s.t.
into	I divided the cookie _____________ two pieces.	**divide** (*this*) _____________ (*that*)
from	They escaped _____________ prison.	**escape** _____________ (*a place*)
about	I heard _____________ the prison escape.	**hear** _____________ s.o./s.t.
from	I heard about it _____________ my cousin.	**hear about** s.t. _____________ s.o.
from	The escapees hid _____________ the police.	**hide** (s.t.) _____________ s.o.
for	We're hoping _____________ good weather.	**hope** _____________ s.t.
by	I multiplied 8 _____________ 2.	**multiply** (*this*) _____________ (*that*)
to / with	I spoke _____________ the teacher.	**speak** _____________ s.o.
about	We spoke to Dr. Carter _____________ my problem.	**speak to/with** _____________ s.t.
about	I told the teacher _____________ my problem.	**tell** s.o. _____________ s.t.
from	I subtracted 7 _____________ 16.	**subtract** (*this*) _____________ (*that*)
about	I wonder _____________ lots of curious things.	**wonder** _____________ s.t.

Preposition Combinations: Group G

PRACTICE 20 ▶ Group G.

Complete the sentences with prepositions.

1. Shhh. I'm trying to concentrate _________ this math problem.

2. How did the bird escape _________ its cage?

3. Did you tell your parents _________ the dent in their new car?

4. We're hoping _________ good weather tomorrow so we can go sailing.

5. Did you hear _________ the earthquake in Turkey?

6. I heard _________ my sister last week. She sent me an email.

7. I spoke _________ Dr. Rice _________ my problem.

8. I'm not accustomed _________ cold weather.

9. When you divide 6 _________ 2, the answer is 3.

10. When you subtract 1 _________ 6, the answer is 5.

11. When you multiply 6 _________ 3, the answer is 18.★

12. When you add 6 _________ 4, the answer is 10.★★

13. George wondered _________ his team's chances of winning the tennis tournament.

14. Zoe hid her journal _________ her younger sister.

★Also possible: multiply 6 times 3
★★Also possible: add 6 and 4; add 6 plus 4

PRACTICE 21 ▶ Groups E, F, and G.

Complete the sentences with prepositions.

1. My father insisted _________ knowing the truth.
2. I was wondering _________ your birthday. What do you want to do?
3. What's the matter _________ you today?
4. She hid the secret _________ everyone.
5. We separated the younger kids _________ the teenagers.
6. I apologized _________ my manager _________ my mistake.
7. We got rid _________ the insects in our apartment.
8. Who does this book belong _________?
9. Does it matter _________ you what time I call this evening?
10. We're looking forward _________ your visit.
11. Fresh vegetables are good _________you.
12. Parents protect their children _________ harm.
13. Shhh. I'm trying to concentrate _________ my work.
14. I rely _________ my friends for their help.
15. I don't approve _________ Bob's lifestyle.
16. The official warned us _________ the danger of traveling alone in the countryside.

Index

Answer Key

CHAPTER 8: CONNECTING IDEAS: PUNCTUATION AND MEANING

PRACTICE 1, p. 127

4. Our amenities include a swimming pool, tennis courts, and a gym.

   noun + noun + noun
5. All rooms have a microwave, refrigerator, and coffee maker.

   noun + noun
6. There is no charge for parking and high-speed internet.

   verb + verb
7. This year we remodeled our hotel and added a new restaurant.

   adjective + adjective
8. Now our guests can enjoy fresh and delicious meals.

   noun + noun
9. We also host weddings and other special events.

   adjective+adjective + adjective
10. Our staff is friendly, helpful, and professional.

PRACTICE 2, p. 127

    S   V   S   V
2a. Dogs bark. Lions roar.

    S   V   S V
2b. Dogs bark, and lions roar.

    S   V   S   V
3a. A week has seven days. A year has 365 days.

    S   V   S   V
3b. A week has seven days, and a year has 365 days.

    S   V   S   V
4a. Ahmed raised his hand, and the teacher pointed at him.

    S   V   S   V
4b. Ahmed raised his hand. The teacher pointed at him.

PRACTICE 3, p. 128

2a. No change.
2b. Their flag is green, black, and yellow.
3a. No change.
3b. Tom made a sandwich, poured a glass of juice, and sat down to eat his lunch.
4a. Ms. Parker is intelligent, friendly, and kind.
4b. No change.
5a. I sent text messages Lily, Daniel, Joe, and Emma.
5b. No change.

5c. Can you watch TV, listen to a podcast, and check text messages at the same time?

PRACTICE 4, p. 128

1a. I Amy jogged along the road. I road my bicycle.
1b. C
2a. C
2b. I My mom trained our dog to sit. My dad trained it to bark at strangers.
3a. I The river rose. It flooded the towns in the valley.
3b. C
4a. C
4b. C
4c. I Sharon's children don't believe in astrology. They don't listen to the information she gives them.

PRACTICE 5, p. 128

Answers may vary.

2. In Japan, many people **live** a long time and **receive** respect when they are old.
3. The twins were **old** and **healthy**.
4. The twins **often** laughed and smiled.
5. The twins **always** had a simple lifestyle and always **walked** everywhere.
6. They **enjoyed** people, and they **enjoyed** each other.
7. Kin and Gin **had many** children **and** grandchildren.
8. When they died, Kin and Gin **weren't** together.

PRACTICE 6, p. 129

3. No change.
4. No change.
5. Please email Jane, Ted, or Anna.
6. Please email Jane, Ted, and Anna.
7. No change.
8. I didn't text Leo, Sarah, or Hugo.
9. I waved at my friend, but she didn't see me.
10. I waved at my friend, and she waved back.

PRACTICE 7, p. 129

1. a	5. e
2. d	6. f
3. g	7. c
4. h	8. b

PRACTICE 8, p. 130

1. c	5. b
2. b	6. c
3. a	7. a
4. c	8. c

PRACTICE 9, p. 130

1. C
2. C
3. C
4. I I bought some apples, peaches, and bananas.
5. I I was hungry, so I ate an apple.
6. C
7. C
8. I My daughter is shy, caring, independent, and smart.

PRACTICE 10, p. 131

1. James has a cold. **H**e needs to rest and drink plenty of fluids, so he should go to bed and drink juice or water. **H**e needs to sleep a lot, so he shouldn't drink fluids with caffeine, such as tea, coffee, or cola.
2. The normal pulse for an adult is between 60 and 80 beats per minute, but exercise, fear, excitement, and a fever will all make a pulse beat faster. **T**he normal pulse for a child is around 80 to 90.
3. Edward Fox was a park ranger for 35 years. **D**uring that time, he was hit by lightning eight times. **T**he lightning never killed him, but it burned his skin and damaged his hearing.

PRACTICE 11, p. 131

Gina wants a job as an air traffic controller. Every air traffic controller worldwide uses English, so it is important for her to become fluent in the language. She has decided to take some intensive English courses at a private language institute, but she isn't sure which one to attend. There are many schools available, and they offer many different kinds of classes. She has also heard of air traffic control schools that include English as part of their coursework, but she needs to have a fairly high level of English to attend. She has to decide soon, or the classes will be full. She's planning to visit her top three choices this summer and decide on the best one for her.

PRACTICE 12, p. 131

2. does
3. didn't
4. do
5. wasn't
6. is
7. will
8. am
9. won't
10. has
11. don't
12. doesn't

PRACTICE 13, p. 132

1. does
2. doesn't
3. isn't
4. are
5. will
6. can
7. would
8. does
9. can't
10. is
11. does
12. did

PRACTICE 14, p. 132

2. does Brian
   Brian doesn't
3. was I
   I was
4. did Jean
   Jean did
5. did Jason
   Jason didn't
6. can Rick
   Rick can't
7. does Laura
   Laura does
8. does Alice
   Alice doesn't

PRACTICE 15, p. 132

Part I

2. doesn't either
3. did too
4. did too
5. couldn't either
6. would too

Part II

8. neither did
9. neither is
10. neither have
11. so did
12. so does

PRACTICE 16, p. 133

2. c
3. b
4. f
5. g
6. d
7. a
8. e

PRACTICE 17, p. 133

2. I opened the window because the room was hot. **A** nice breeze came in.
3. Because the weather was bad, we canceled our trip into the city. **W**e stayed home and watched TV.
4. Gabi loves gymnastics. **B**ecause she hopes to be on an Olympic team, she practices hard every day.
5. Francisco is very good in math. **B**ecause several colleges want him to attend, they are offering him full scholarships.

PRACTICE 18, p. 134

2. *didn't have money*—The family couldn't buy food because they didn't have money.
3. *work long hours*—Because our neighbors work long hours, they aren't home very much.
4. *be tired*—Because I am tired, I am going to bed.
5. *exercise every day*—Because Sofia exercises every day, she is in great shape.
6. *have a high fever*—Because Jennifer has a high fever, she is going to the doctor.

PRACTICE 19, p. 134

1. c. He ate a sandwich **because** he was hungry.
2. a. **Because** my sister was tired, she went to bed.
   b. My sister went to bed **because** she was tired.
   c. My sister was tired, **so** she went to bed.
3. a. Sam worked hard, **so** he got a promotion.
   b. **Because** he worked hard, Sam got a promotion.
   c. Sam got a promotion **because** he worked hard.
4. a. Olivia has a meeting, **so** she'll be home late tonight.
   b. Olivia will be home late tonight **because** she has a meeting.
   c. **Because** she has a meeting, Olivia will be home late tonight.
5. a. Students can usually identify Italy easily on a world map **because** it is shaped like a boot.
   b. **Because** Italy has the distinctive shape of a boot, students can usually identify it easily.
   c. Italy has the distinctive shape of a boot, **so** students can usually identify it easily on a map.

PRACTICE 20, p. 135

3. is
4. stayed
5. didn't change
6. didn't pass
7. ate
8. were

1. b
2. a
3. a
4. b
5. a
6. a
7. b
8. b

PRACTICE 22, p. 136

2. even though
3. even though
4. even though
5. because
6. Even though
7. Because
8. Even though
9. Even though
10. Because

PRACTICE 23, p. 136

1. because
2. because
3. although
4. Because
5. Although
6. although
7. because

PRACTICE 24, p. 137

2. a
3. c
4. b
5. b
6. c
7. b
8. b
9. a
10. c

PRACTICE 25, p. 138

2. The flight was overbooked, **so** I had to fly on another airline. OR **Because** the flight was overbooked, I had to fly on another airline.
3. Many people use their phones to post pictures on social media, check email, and watch videos.
4. Even **though** my father works two jobs, he always has time to play soccer or baseball on the weekends with his family.
5. I saw a bad accident, and my sister **did** too.
6. Oscar always pays his bills on time, but his brother **doesn't**.
7. **Although** / **Even though** my mother is afraid of heights, I took her up to the observation deck at the top of the building. OR Because … I **didn't take** her …
8. Janey doesn't like to get up early, and **Joe doesn't either** / **neither does Joe**.
9. My mother and my father **immigrated** to this country 30 years ago.
10. **Because** Maya is very intelligent, her parents want to put her in an advanced program at school.

PRACTICE 26, p. 139

but
although
because
and
too
either
or
neither
so

CHAPTER 9: COMPARISONS

PRACTICE 1, p. 140

1. larger
2. closer
3. hotter
4. colder
5. heavier
6. more intelligent
7. worse
8. better

PRACTICE 2, p. 140

2. more expensive than
3. larger
4. hotter than
5. slower than
6. creamier than
7. worse than
8. faster than
9. more important
10. quicker than
11. heavier
12. older than
13. shorter than
14. heavier than
15. more expensive than

PRACTICE 3, p. 141

2. foggier … sunnier
3. drier … healthier
4. more international … more expensive … cheaper

PRACTICE 4, p. 141

2. the biggest organ
3. the most common word
4. the closest planet
5. the largest continent
6. the most intelligent animals
7. the worst floods, the highest level
8. the best policy

PRACTICE 5, p. 141

3. the best
4. better
5. the worst
6. worse
7. the worst
8. better

PRACTICE 6, p. 142

3. softer … the softest
4. lazier … the laziest
5. more wonderful … the most wonderful
6. calmer … the calmest
7. lower … the lowest
8. thinner … the thinnest
9. more convenient … the most convenient
10. more simple / simpler … the most simple / the simplest
11. better … the best
12. worse … the worst
13. more famous … the most famous
14. slower … the slowest
15. more slowly … the most slowly

PRACTICE 7, p. 142

3. she did / her
4. I was / me
5. he will / him
6. he has / him
7. I am / me
8. he is / him
9. I am / me
10. she is / her

PRACTICE 8, p. 143

Part I

2. the easiest … ever
3. the most interesting … in
4. the best … of
5. the wisest … ever
6. the fastest … of
7. the most brilliant … in
8. the most successful … in
9. the busiest … in
10. the most generous … ever
11. the most important … in
12. the most artistic of

PRACTICE 9, p. 144

3. more serious (adj)
4. more seriously (adv)
5. more politely (adv)
6. more polite (adj)
7. more careful (adj)
8. more carefully (adv)
9. more clearly (adv)
10. clearer (adj)

PRACTICE 10, p. 145

1. a, b
2. b
3. a, b
4. b
5. b
6. a, b

PRACTICE 11, p. 145

2. bigger and bigger
3. warmer and warmer
4. noisier and noisier
5. madder and madder
6. longer and longer
7. more and more expensive
8. friendlier and friendlier / more and more friendly
9. worse and worse

PRACTICE 12, p. 146

2. softer … easier
3. simpler … more relaxed
4. longer … more tired
5. harder … more

PRACTICE 13, p. 146

1. more she talked, the more excited she got
2. more he talked, the hungrier I got
3. the older you are, the more you understand
4. faster he talked, the more confused I became
5. the more the fans clapped and cheered, the better their team played

PRACTICE 14, p. 146

1. a
2. b, c, d
3. a
4. b, c, d
5. b, c, d
6. a
7. b, c, d
8. a
9. b, c, d

PRACTICE 15, p. 147

2. b
3. b
4. a
5. a
6. b
7. a
8. b

PRACTICE 16, p. 148

2. sadder … the saddest
3. the best … better
4. more exhausting … the most exhausting
5. happier … the happiest
6. more entertaining … the most entertaining
7. harder … the hardest
8. hotter … the hottest

PRACTICE 17, p. 148

3. (nearly) as tired as Susan (was).
4. (nearly) as tired as Susan (was).
5. (just) as lazy as her sister Amanda (is).
6. (nearly) as lazy as Alan (is).

PRACTICE 18, p. 149

2. is as tall as
3. isn't as wealthy as
4. isn't as polluted as
5. isn't as studious as
6. aren't as difficult as

PRACTICE 19, p. 149

2. almost as / not quite as
3. not nearly as
4. just as

Part II

6. not nearly as
7. almost as / not quite as
8. not nearly as

Part III

9. just as
10. not nearly as
11. almost as / not quite as

Part IV

12. just as
13. almost as
14. just as
15. not nearly as
16. almost as / not quite as

PRACTICE 20, p. 151

Part I

2. as ice
3. as a picture
4. as a bat
5. as a bone
6. as a pillow
7. as a wink
8. as a mouse
9. as a bird
10. as ABC

Part II

12. quick as a wink
13. blind as a bat
14. white as snow
15. quiet as a mouse
16. pretty as a picture
17. simple as ABC
18. free as a bird
19. soft as a pillow
20. dry as dust

PRACTICE 21, p. 152

not as interesting as → less interesting than
not as difficult → less difficult
not as convenient as → less convenient than
not as close to (no change)
not as exciting as → less exciting than
not as comfortable → less comfortable
not as unhappy as → less unhappy than
not as bad as (no change)

PRACTICE 22, p. 152

1. more students
2. more money
3. more vegetables
4. more sugar
5. more days
6. more space
7. more paper
8. more time
9. more water
10. more winter clothes

PRACTICE 23, p. 153

Part I. Adjectives

1. more pleasant
2. louder
3. more difficult

 Adverbs
  4. more clearly
  5. more carefully
  6. faster

Part III. Nouns
  7. more homework
  8. more snow
  9. more friends
  10. more problems
  11. more cars
  12. more money

PRACTICE 24, p. 154

1. c   6. a
2. c   7. b
3. c   8. c
4. a   9. a
5. b   10. c

PRACTICE 25, p. 154

2. the most popular … in
3. smaller than
4. More potatoes … than
5. the closest … faster than
6. the largest … in … the smallest … of
7. more information
8. kinder … more generous
9. more honest … than
10. the worst
11. the safest
12. faster … than
13. bigger than

PRACTICE 26, p. 155

3. alike   7. alike
4. alike   8. like
5. like   9. like
6. like   10. alike

PRACTICE 27, p. 155

2. similar to   7. the same as
3. the same as   8. different from
4. different from   9. similar to
5. the same as   10. different from
6. similar to

PRACTICE 28, p. 156

2. A and D are alike.
3. C is similar to A and D.
4. B is different from A, C, and D.

Part II
5. similar to
6. the same as
7. different
8. the same as
9. different from

PRACTICE 29, p. 156

2. like
3. alike
4. A: alike
   B: the same … the same … the same

5. like
6. A: like
   B: similar
7. alike … alike … different
8. the same … the same … different

PRACTICE 30, p. 157

2. A sea is **deeper** than a lake.
3. A donkey isn't as big **as** a horse.
4. Ellen is **the** happiest person I've ever met.
5. When I feel embarrassed, my face gets **hotter and hotter**.
6. One of **the** largest **animals** in the world is the hippopotamus.
7. The traffic on the highway is **worse** than it used to be.
8. Jack is the same **age as** Jerry / **as old as** Jerry.
9. Peas are similar **to** beans, but they have several differences.
10. Last winter was pretty mild. This winter is cold and rainy. It's much **rainier** than last winter.
11. Mrs. Peters, the substitute teacher, is **friendlier** than the regular instructor.
12. Although alligators and crocodiles are similar, alligators are **not as big as** / **smaller than** crocodiles.
13. Mohammed and Tarek come from different countries, but they became friends easily because they speak **the** same language, Arabic.
14. Leah and Kate are sisters. They look a lot **alike**, but Leah is **taller** than Kate.
15. Ramzy is an excellent student. He is the **best** student in his class.
16. I ordered a new dress. I like it, but it doesn't look **like** the picture online.
17. Abby wears a different pair of shoes every day. She owns more shoes **than** anyone I know.
18. San Francisco is a very windy city. Is it **as** windy as Chicago?

PRACTICE 31, p. 158

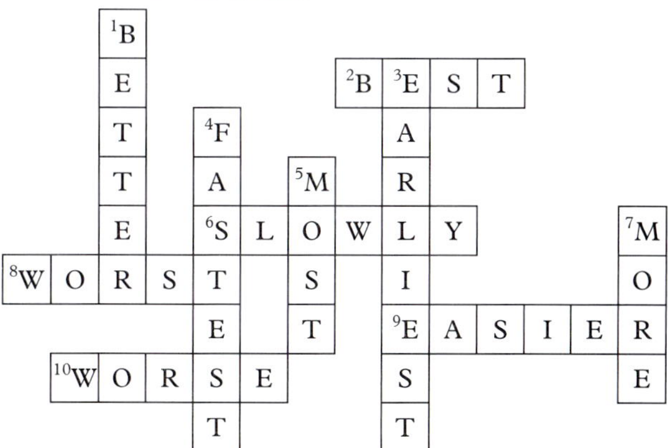

CHAPTER 10: THE PASSIVE

PRACTICE 1, p. 159

3. active, posted
4. passive, was posted
5. active, explained
6. passive, was explained
7. passive, are designed
8. active, design

 9. active, is fixing
10. passive, is being fixed

PRACTICE 2, p. 159
2. was delivered
3. has been delivered
4. is going to be delivered
5. will be delivered

PRACTICE 3, p. 160
2. built
3. bought
4. carried
5. done
6. eaten
7. found
8. given
9. gone
10. grown
11. hit
12. hurt
13. left
14. lost
15. fed
16. made
17. planned
18. played
19. pulled
20. read
21. saved
22. sent
23. spoken
24. spent
25. taken
26. taught
27. visited
28. worn
29. written
30. invited

PRACTICE 4, p. 160
2. are written
3. are read
4. was built
5. were found
6. has been eaten
7. is going to be visited
8. will be played
9. are going to be taken
10. have been grown
11. haven't been fed
12. weren't invited

PRACTICE 5, p. 160
2. are flown
3. are led
4. is followed

6. was shot
7. were made
8. was discovered

10. has been written
11. has been bought
12. have been arrested

14. will be taken
15. will be elected
16. will be won

18. are going to be taught
19. are going to be hired
20. is going to be sent

PRACTICE 6, p. 161

Part I
2. are written
3. is grown
4. are eaten
5. am paid
6. is understood

Part II
8. was built
9. were written
10. was destroyed

Part III
12. has been spoken
13. has been read
14. has been worn

Part IV
16. will be visited
17. will be saved

Part V
19. are going to be offered
20. is going to be chosen

PRACTICE 7, p. 162
2. b
3. b
4. a
5. b
6. a
7. b

PRACTICE 8, p. 163
2. Movie critics have reviewed the film.
3. Audiences gave the movie good ratings.
4. Did a famous writer write the movie?
5. An unknown actor plays the lead role.
6. Does someone commit a murder in the movie?
7. Does a spy kill the main character?
8. Will many people see the movie?
9. Is the movie going to win an award?

PRACTICE 9, p. 163
2. was being held
3. were being taken
4. is being used
5. are being ordered
6. are being answered

PRACTICE 10, p. 164
2. The oil was being changed.
3. The tire pressure was being checked.
4. Windshield wiper fluid was being added.
5. New brake pads are being installed.
6. A broken headlight is being replaced.
7. The transmission is being repaired.
8. The tires are being balanced and rotated.

PRACTICE 11, p. 165
2. Will Pat be shocked by the news?
3. Is lunch being served by the restaurant now?
4. Are the rules understood by everyone?
5. Is the solution going to be explained by the professor?
6. Have you been accepted by the university?
7. Has the contract been signed by both the buyer and the seller?
8. Was the suspect found by the police?
9. Are you being helped?
10. Has the package been delivered yet?

PRACTICE 12, p. 165
3. transitive   groceries
4. intransitive   no object
5. transitive   the ball
6. intransitive   no object

7. intransitive   no object   10. intransitive   no object
8. transitive   a snake   11. intransitive   no object
9. transitive   the book   12. transitive   his keys

PRACTICE 13, p. 166

3. a tree; A tree was struck by lightning.
4. No change.
5. my neighbor's car; My neighbor's car was hit by the tree.
6. the car alarm; The car alarm was set off by the impact.
7. No change.
8. the roof of the car; The roof of the car was damaged by the tree.
9. No change.

PRACTICE 14, p. 166

Checked sentences: 2, 4, 6, 9

PRACTICE 15, p. 166

	passive verb	**action performed by**
3.	will be translated	unknown
4.	was stolen	unknown
5.	was designed	a famous architect
6.	is going to be built	unknown
7.	has been rented	a young family with two small children
8.	has also been rented	unknown

PRACTICE 16, p. 167

3. Ethnic dishes are served at that restaurant.
4. I was confused in class yesterday.
5. I was confused by the teacher's directions.
6. The dishes haven't been washed yet.
7. They will be washed soon.
8. Was this sweater washed in hot water?
9. I was invited to the party by Luis.
10. Have you been invited to the party?

PRACTICE 17, p. 168

3. Students are taught by teachers.
4. Students study a lot.
5. Cereal is often eaten at breakfast.
6. Kate feeds the cat every day.
7. The cat is fed by Kate every day.
8. Songs are sung to children by their mothers.
9. Thai food is cooked in Thai restaurants.
10. Chefs cook in restaurants.

PRACTICE 18, p. 168

2. b		6. a
3. a		7. b
4. b		8. a
5. b		

PRACTICE 19, p. 169

3. I I went to school yesterday.
4. I Two firefighters were injured while they were fighting the fire.
5. I Sara accidentally broke the window.
6. C (No change.)
7. I Tim was eating when his phone rang.
8. I I agree with you.
9. I The little boy fell down while he was running in the park.
10. I The swimmer died from a shark attack.
11. C (No change.)
12. I I slept for nine hours last night.

PRACTICE 20, p. 169

2. should be returned
3. must be paid
4. could be sent
5. should be sent
6. can be put away
7. may be thrown away
8. might be picked up
9. will be cleaned up

PRACTICE 21, p. 170

2. a. No, the last paragraph has to be changed.
   b. No, it must be signed by Mr. Hayes.
3. a. It might be bought by a famous hockey star.
   b. It may be turned into apartments.
4. a. The credit card company should be called immediately.
   b. The mistake ought to be fixed right away.
5. a. It should be read by everyone.
   b. A movie of the book will be made.
6. a. It should be shortened.
   b. It has to be done soon.
7. a. It should be reported to the police.
   b. Your credit cards have to be canceled.

PRACTICE 22, p. 171

1. appeared … were made … were worn … began … were called … became … remained … were put … wore … have been manufactured
2. were being sold … checked … weren't needed … might disappear …. could be considered
3. become…is being replaced … feature … offer … can use … can be downloaded … can be managed … include … are designed

PRACTICE 23, p. 171

Part I

2. about
3. from
4. of
5. in / with
6. of
7. with
8. in / with
9. about
10. with

Part II

11. in
12. with
13. of
14. to
15. to
16. with
17. from

Part III

18. of
19. in
20. with
21. for

2. Mr. and Mrs. Rose **are** devoted to each other.
3. Could you please help me? I need directions. I **am** lost.
4. The students are **bored with** their chemistry project.
5. The paper bags at this store **are composed of** recycled products.
6. Your friend needs a doctor. He **is** hurt.
7. How well are you **prepared for** the driver's license test?
8. Mary has been engage**d to** Paul for five years. Will they ever get married?

PRACTICE 25, p. 172

2. interested
3. exciting
4. excited
5. fascinated
6. fascinating
7. boring … confusing
8. bored … confused
9. interesting
10. fascinating … surprising; also possible: surprising … fascinating

PRACTICE 26, p. 173

2. confusing … confused
3. excited … exciting
4. surprising … surprised
5. embarrassing … embarrassed
6. fascinating … fascinated

PRACTICE 27, p. 173

2. a
3. b
4. a
5. c

PRACTICE 28, p. 174

2. embarrassing
3. interested
4. interesting
5. exhausting … tired
6. exhausting
7. frightening
8. frightened
9. confusing
10. confused … frustrated

PRACTICE 29, p. 174

1. g
2. c
3. a
4. h
5. b
6. f
7. d
8. e

PRACTICE 30, p. 175

3. am getting
4. got
5. Get
6. get
7. got
8. get
9. am getting
10. am getting

PRACTICE 31, p. 175

2. a
3. b, c
4. a
5. a
6. b, c
7. b, c
8. a

PRACTICE 32, p. 176

3. are … am
4. Ø
5. is
6. Ø
7. Ø
8. is
9. is
10. Ø

PRACTICE 33, p. 176

2. is used to working
3. used to play
4. used to be
5. is used to working
6. is used to eating

PRACTICE 34, p. 176

2. We are supposed to read Chapter 9 before class tomorrow.
3. I was supposed to go to a party last night, but I stayed home.
4. We are supposed to do Exercise 10 for homework.
5. It is supposed to rain tomorrow.
6. I am / you are supposed to take one pill every six hours.
7. I am supposed to dust the furniture and vacuum the carpet.

PRACTICE 35, P. 177

2. My uncle died in the war.
3. Miami is located in Florida.
4. I was very worried about my son.
5. Mr. Rivera is interested in finding a new career.
6. Did you tell everyone the shocking news?
7. After ten years, I am finally used to this wet and rainy climate.
8. The newspaper is supposed to come every morning before eight.
9. The Millers have been married to each other for 60 years.
10. I used to drink coffee with cream, but now I drink it black.
11. What happened at the party last night?
12. Several people almost got killed when the fireworks exploded over them.
13. A new parking garage is being built for our office.
14. I have been living in England for several years, so I am accustomed to driving on the left side of the road.

PRACTICE 36, p. 177

was hit … are used to … was destroyed … was torn off … fell … lost … feel … injured … left … caring …. was insured … being … are being replaced … should

CHAPTER 11: COUNT/NONCOUNT NOUNS AND ARTICLES

PRACTICE 1, p. 178

2. an
3. a
4. an
5. a
6. a
7. an
8. a
9. an
10. an
11. an
12. a
13. a
14. an
15. a
16. a
17. an
18. a
19. an
20. a
21. a
22. an

PRACTICE 2, p. 178

1. a chair
2. chairs
3. chairs
4. chair
5. furniture
6. Some
7. Furniture
8. some
9. desk
10. desks

PRACTICE 3, p. 179

Baggage	Fruit	Jewelry	Furniture
backpacks	apples	bracelets	beds
handbags	bananas	earrings	chairs
purses	oranges	necklaces	sofas
suitcases	strawberries	rings	tables

PRACTICE 4, p. 179

1. water
2. light
3. thunder
4. gold
5. help
6. fun

PRACTICE 5, p. 179

1. Ø … Ø
2. Ø … boots … socks
3. cookies … Ø
4. Ø … Ø … Ø
5. Ø … bones
6. Ø … Ø
7. Ø … Ø

PRACTICE 6, p. 180

3. Ø   slang
4. Ø   homework
5. assignment   assignments
6. dress   dresses
7. Ø   clothing
8. family   families
9. Ø   knowledge
10. Ø   information
11. fact   facts
12. Ø   luck
13. cup   cups
14. Ø   coffee
15. question   questions

PRACTICE 7, p. 180

1. Tom lived in **a** big city for many years. However, three years ago he left the city. It had Ø pollution and Ø smog, and he couldn't breathe well. Now he lives in **a** small town in the mountains. He breathes Ø clean air and drinks Ø fresh water. He knows that it was **a** good idea to leave the city because his health is better.

2. Cornell University is named for Ezra Cornell. Ezra Cornell was a philanthropist who lived in Ithaca, New York. He loved the area and wanted to improve it. People there didn't have **a** library, and so he built one for them. Then, he wanted to build **a** university where people could gain Ø knowledge in Ø practical subjects, such as farming, as well as in Ø history, Ø literature, and Ø science. Cornell owned **a** large farm in the area, and in an act of generosity, he donated it as the site for the new university. Cornell University opened in 1865, and today it is known as **an** excellent university — one of the best universities in the world.

PRACTICE 8, p. 181

1. bread, corn, peas, and rice.
2. apple trees, grass, lakes, mountains, and scenery.
3. equipment, machines, machinery, and tools.
4. bracelets, jewels, jewelry, and rings.

PRACTICE 9, p. 181

1. one
2. much
3. many
4. much
5. much
6. much
7. much
8. many
9. one
10. much
11. many
12. much
13. much
14. one
15. many
16. many

PRACTICE 10, p. 181

1. a. apples, vegetables
   b. coffee, fruit, sugar
2. a. answers, people, things
   b. English, slang
3. a. ideas, suggestions
   b. homework, information, work
4. a. police officers
   b. crime, garbage, traffic, violence

PRACTICE 11, p. 182

4. much English literature Ø
5. many English words
6. much gasoline Ø
7. much petrol Ø
8. many grandchildren
9. much fun Ø
10. many islands are
11. many people Ø
12. many zeroes / zeros are

PRACTICE 12, p. 182

3. a
4. some, much
5. some, many
6. some, much
7. an
8. a
9. an
10. some, many
11. a
12. an
13. some, many
14. some, much
15. a
16. some, much
17. a
18. an
19. some, much
20. some, many

PRACTICE 13, p. 183

2. a little … Ø
3. a few oranges
4. a little … Ø
5. a little … Ø
6. a few suggestions
7. a few questions
8. a few … Ø
9. a few … minutes
10. a little … Ø
11. a little … Ø
12. a little … Ø

PRACTICE 14, p. 183

1. a, b, c, e
2. a, b, d, f, g, h
3. a, b, e
4. a, b, d, e
5. b, d, e, g
6. a, b, c, e, f, h

PRACTICE 15, p. 184
(1) Scientists ... animals ... plants ... place
(2) flowers ... trees ... deserts ... oceans ... mountains
(3) Rice ... crop ... world ... crops ... weather ... fields
(4) Plants ... health ... air ... trees ... earth ... air

PRACTICE 16, p. 185
1. f
2. b
3. h
4. j
5. i
6. d
7. g
8. a
9. c
10. e

PRACTICE 17, p. 185

Common answers:
2. bottle
3. box / bag
4. jar / bottle
5. can
6. bag / box
7. jar
8. bottle
9. bag / box
10. can / bag

PRACTICE 18, p. 185
3. glass, cup
4. gallons
5. bottle / carton
6. carton
7. pieces
8. piece
9. sheets / pieces
10. loaf
11. piece
12. piece

PRACTICE 19, p. 186
3. many pairs of sandals
4. much toothpaste
5. much luggage
6. much money
7. many days

PRACTICE 20, p. 186
2. non-specific
3. non-specific
4. specific
5. specific
6. non-specific

PRACTICE 21, p. 187
1. the ... the ... the ... the ... the ... the
2. Ø ... the ... Ø ... the ... the
3. Ø ... Ø ... Ø ... Ø ... Ø ... an ... the ... a ... The ...
   Ø ... the ... the

PRACTICE 22, p. 187
3. a ... a ... a
4. the ... the
5. the
6. a
7. a ... a
8. the ... the
9. the
10. a
11. a ... a
12. The ... the ... the
13. a
14. the

PRACTICE 23, p. 188
1. some ... a ... The ... the
2. some ... a ... a ... a ... The ... The ... the
3. A: an
   A: A ... a ... a
   B: the
   A: The ... the ... the
4. a ... a ... an ... The ... the ... the ... the ... the

PRACTICE 24, p. 189
2. a
3. a
4. The
5. a
6. the
7. the
8. the
9. the
10. the
11. a
12. the
13. the
14. the
15. the
16. a
17. the
18. the
19. the

PRACTICE 25, p. 190
1. a ... Ø ... Ø
2. Ø
3. The
4. The ... a ... the ... Ø ... Ø ... Ø
5. A: the
   B: the
6. Ø ... The ... a ... the ... an ... a
7. Ø ... Ø ... Ø
8. A: the
   B: the ... the
9. an ... A ... a ... a ... Ø ... the ... the ... the

PRACTICE 26, p. 190
3. Ø ... the
4. The ... Ø
5. Ø ... Ø
6. Ø ... Ø
7. Ø
8. The ... Ø ... Ø
9. Ø
10. Ø ... Ø ... Ø
11. The
12. The ... Ø ... The ... the

PRACTICE 27, p. 191
2. **the** Amazon River
3. Shanghai
4. **the** Sahara Desert
5. **the** Thames River
6. Europe
7. **the** Alps
8. Lake Tanganyika
9. North America
10. **the** Indian Ocean
11. **the** Netherlands
12. North America
13. Nepal
14. **the** Urals
15. Lagos
16. **the** United Arab Emirates

PRACTICE 28, p. 192
2. I'm taking history, biology, **E**nglish, and calculus this semester.
3. Some lab classes meet on **S**aturday.
4. My roommate likes **V**ietnamese food, and **I** like **T**hai food.
5. Shelia works for the **X**erox corporation. **I**t is a very large corporation.
6. Pedro is from **L**atin **A**merica. He speaks **S**panish.
7. My favorite park is **C**entral **P**ark in **N**ew **Y**ork.
8. No change.
9. I like **U**ncle **J**oe and **A**unt **S**ara.
10. **S**usan **W**. **M**iller is a professor.
11. I am in **P**rof. **M**iller's class.
12. In **J**anuary, it's winter in **C**anada and summer in **A**rgentina.

13. I would like to visit **L**os **A**ngeles.
14. It's the largest city in **C**alifornia.

PRACTICE 29, p. 192

1. The mail carrier brought only one **letter** today.
2. Mr. Dale gave his class **a** long history assignment for the weekend.
3. Tariq speaks several language**s**, including Arabic and German.
4. I usually have **a** glass **of** water with my lunch.
5. A helpful police officer gave us (**some**) **information** about the city.
6. This recipe calls for two cup**s** of nut**s**.
7. **Many** vegetable**s** are believed to have cancer-fighting ingredients.
8. Only applicants with the necessary **experience** should apply for the computer position.
9. When Vicki likes a movie, she sees it several time**s**.
10. No change.
11. Is it possible to stop all **violence** in the world?
12. Some of the **homework** for my English class was easy, but many of the assignment**s** were unclear.
13. Diane has been to Hong Kong several time**s** recently. She always has **a** wonderful time.
14. Many parents need **advice** about raising children.
15. A person doesn't need **much** equipment to play baseball: just **a** ball and a bat.
16. I usually go to school in the morning, and I work in **the** afternoon.
17. Do you have any **advice** for new students?
18. The beaches in my country have beautiful **sand**.

PRACTICE 30, p. 193

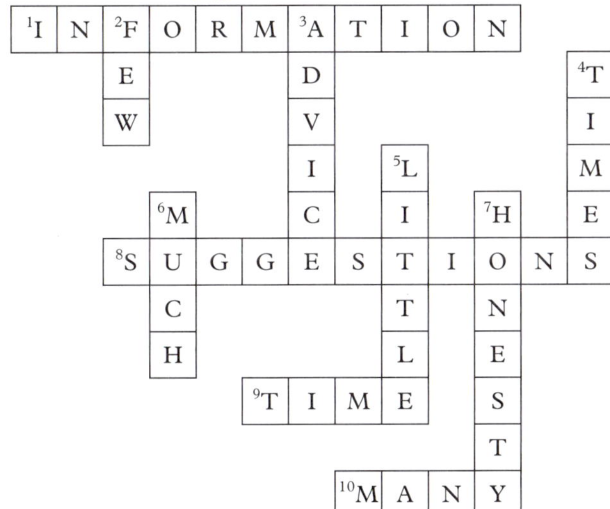

CHAPTER 12: ADJECTIVE CLAUSES

PRACTICE 1, p. 194

Check 1, 2, 5, 6, 7

PRACTICE 2, p. 194

2. who was wearing a gray suit
   1: A woman asked
   2: She was wearing
3. that was wearing a blue coat
   1: I saw
   2: He was wearing
4. who had pulled his brother from the icy river
   1: The parents hugged
   2: He had pulled
5. that broke the vase
   1: The girl apologized
   2: She broke

PRACTICE 3, p. 195

Adjective clauses:

    S   V
2. who live across the street
    S   V
3. that is from India
    S   V
4. who have children
    S   V
5. who teaches at the university
    S   V
6. who is training to play basketball in the Special Olympics.

PRACTICE 4, p. 195

2. *Complex sentence 1:* The man who played the guitar is also a singer.
   Complex sentence 2: The man that played the guitar is also a singer.
3. Complex *sentence 1:* I read about the soccer player who was injured yesterday.
   Complex sentence 2: I read about the soccer player that was injured yesterday.
4. Complex *sentence 1:* I know a man who has sailed around the world.
   Complex sentence 2: I know a man that has sailed around the world.

PRACTICE 5, p. 196

2. who / that makes pizza
3. who / that plays tennis
4. who / that teaches English
5. who / that trains horses
6. who / that eats meat
7. who / that drink tea
8. who / that fight fires

PRACTICE 6, p. 196

2. The woman Jack saw was very tall.
3. The woman that Jack knows is a professor.
4. The student that the teacher helped was grateful.
5. The student I helped was happy about the exam.
6. The student who I just met won a scholarship.
7. The student whom you see over there is the class president.

PRACTICE 7, p. 197

3. S	8. O that
4. O that	9. S
5. S	10. O that
6. S	11. S
7. O that	

1. a, b, c, d
2. c, d
3. a, b, c, d
4. c, d
5. b, d
6. a, b, c

PRACTICE 9, p. 198

3. that, Ø, who
4. that, who
5. that, who
6. that, Ø, who

PRACTICE 10, p. 198

2. a
3. b
4. b
5. a
6. a
7. b
8. b

PRACTICE 11, p. 199

3. O that
4. O that
5. S
6. S
7. S
8. O that

PRACTICE 12, p. 199

2. that / which
3. that / which / Ø
4. that / which / Ø
5. that / which

PRACTICE 13, p. 199

2. that I drank
3. I was wearing
4. that I've known and loved
5. who I married
6. that we have had
7. which we bought

PRACTICE 14, p. 200

2. a, c
3. c, d
4. c, d, e
5. a, c
6. c, d, e
7. a, b, c, e
8. c, d, e
9. a, c
10. c, d

PRACTICE 15, p. 201

2. people ... are
3. compound ... consists
4. students ... speak
5. people ... know
6. student ... is
7. people ... live
8. person ... makes
9. artists ... make

PRACTICE 16, p. 201

2. a. you introduced me to
   b. you introduced me to
3. a. I am quite familiar with
   b. which I am quite familiar
4. a. you should talk with
   b. whom you should talk
5. a. we are waiting for
   b. we are waiting for
6. a. I'm interested in
   b. I'm interested in

PRACTICE 17, p. 202

2. a. that ... to
   b. which ... to
   c. Ø ... to
   d. which ... Ø
3. a. that ... in
   b. which ... in
   c. Ø ... in
   d. which ... Ø
4. a. that ... with
   b. Ø ... with
   c. who ... with
   d. that ... with
   e. whom ... Ø

PRACTICE 18, p. 202

3. The bus [we were waiting **for**] was only three minutes late.
4. Mrs. Chan is someone [I always enjoy talking **to** about politics.]
5. I showed my roommate the text message [I got from a co-worker Ø.]
6. One of the subjects [I've been interested **in** for a long time] is astronomy.
7. The people [I talked **to** at the reception] were interesting.
8. One of the places [I want to visit Ø next year] is Mexico City.
9. The website [I was looking **at**] had useful reviews of local restaurants.
10. The book [I wanted Ø] wasn't available at the library.
11. English grammar is one of the subjects [Ø which I enjoy studying the most.]
12. The friend [I waved **to** / **at**] didn't wave back. Maybe he just didn't see me.

PRACTICE 19, p. 203

2. whose husband is out of work
   1: The woman found a job at JJ's Diner.
   2: Her husband is out of work.
3. whose wallet I found
   1: The man gave me a reward.
   2: I found his wallet.

PRACTICE 20, p. 203

2.   His
   → I talked to the boy whose kite was caught in a tree.
3.   Their
   → The family whose house burned down is staying in a motel.
4.   Her
   → I talked to a woman whose parents know my parents.
5.   Her
   → The reporter whose articles explained global warming won an award.
6.   His
   → I know a man whose daughter entered college at the age of 14.
7.   Her
   → We observed a language teacher whose teaching methods included role-playing.
8.   Their
   → The teachers whose methods include role-playing are very popular.

PRACTICE 21, p. 204

2. c
3. b, c
4. c
5. a
6. a, c

2. who / that
3. that / which / Ø
4. whose
5. that / which
6. Ø / that / who / whom
7. whose
8. that / which
9. who / that
10. Ø / that / who / whom
11. who / that … Ø / that / who / whom … whom

PRACTICE 23, p. 205

1. a
2. b
3. b
4. b
5. a
6. a
7. a
8. b

PRACTICE 24, p. 206

2. My family lived in a house **that / which was** built in 1900.
3. There's the man that we saw on TV.
4. I don't know people **whose** lives are carefree.
5. It is important to help people who **have** no money.
6. At the airport, I was waiting for friends Ø / that / who / whom I hadn't seen for a long time.
7. The woman **who / that** lives next door likes to relax by doing crossword puzzles every evening.
8. My teacher has two cats **whose** names are Ping and Pong.
9. I enjoyed the songs which we sang.
10. The person **to whom** you should speak is Gary Green.

PRACTICE 25, p. 206

1. whom
2. who
3. whose
4. which
5. that

CHAPTER 13: GERUNDS AND INFINITIVES

PRACTICE 1, p. 207

2. living
3. taking
4. buying
5. giving
6. doing
7. reviewing
8. finding
9. driving
10. retiring
11. getting married
12. working

PRACTICE 2, p. 207

2. is going to go hiking
3. went shopping
4. go swimming
5. goes fishing
6. go sightseeing
7. go camping
8. go sailing
9. go skiing
10. went skydiving

PRACTICE 3, p. 208

3. to help   INF
4. cleaning   GER
5. to order   INF
6. quitting   GER
7. to work   INF
8. to grow   INF

PRACTICE 4, p. 208

2. being
3. to pay

4. mailing
5. to pass
6. to consider
7. accepting
8. reading
9. swimming
10. to hurt
11. asking
12. to look
13. to try
14. to enjoy
15. opening
16. to keep
17. to give
18. to support
19. to finish
20. to visit

PRACTICE 5, p. 209

3. a, b
4. b
5. a, b
6. a, b
7. a, b
8. b
9. a
10. a, b
11. a, b
12. a, b
13. b
14. a
15. b

PRACTICE 6, p. 210

1. to go … to pay … to get … to apply … to receive
2. to take . . to go … to go … being … to go … skiing … swimming … sailing
3. getting … to tell … leaving … to have … to create … to take

PRACTICE 7, p. 211

Part I
3. to work
4. working
5. to work
6. to work / working
7. to work
8. to work
9. working
10. to work
11. to work
12. working

Part II
13. to leave
14. to leave
15. leaving
16. leaving
17. leaving
18. leaving
19. to leave
20. to leave
21. leaving
22. to leave

Part III
23. to know
24. to know
25. to know
26. knowing
27. to know
28. to know
29. to know / knowing
30. to know
31. to know
32. to know / knowing

PRACTICE 8, p. 211

Part I
2. for hurting
3. in helping
4. at listening
5. of working
6. about walking
7. of / about owning
8. about buying

Part II
9. for closing
10. for lending
11. on becoming
12. for taking
13. on eating
14. to finishing
15. from making
16. about … having

PRACTICE 9, p. 212

2. in … in learning
3. for … for helping
4. on … on walking
5. for … for losing

6. like ... like going
7. at ... at drawing
8. in ... in saving
9. about ... about
   forgetting

10. about ... about going
11. to ... to going
12. of ... of staying

PRACTICE 10, p. 213

Part I
2. f
3. a
4. b

5. c
6. d

Part II
7. j
8. k
9. l

10. g
11. h
12. i

PRACTICE 11, p. 214

(1) doing ... doing / to do ... to do
(2) to write ... doing ... thinking
(3) for being ... to thank ... sending ... wearing ... to wear
(4) to seeing ... for taking

PRACTICE 12, p. 214

2. to eat
3. to pick
3. waiting
4. about being
5. to choose
6. playing / to play
7. having
8. of walking
9. on paying

PRACTICE 13, p. 215

2. by reading
3. by telling
4. by watching

5. by running
6. by treating

PRACTICE 14, p. 215

2. by pouring
3. by stretching
4. by working
5. by saving

6. by following
7. by looking
8. by counting

PRACTICE 15, p. 216

1. a, d, e, f
2. a, b, c
3. b, c, d, f
4. a, b, d, e, f

PRACTICE 16, p. 216

2. a. Eating ... is
   b. It is ... to eat
3. a. Driving ... is
   b. It is ... to drive
4. a. It is ... to travel
   b. Traveling ... is
5. a. Is it ... to live
   b. Is living
6. a. Is it ... to complete
   b. Is completing

PRACTICE 17, p. 216

2. it is customary for young children to sleep ...
3. It is necessary for airline pilots to have ...
4. It is hard for many teenagers to wake up ...
5. It is important for elderly people to keep ...
6. It is boring for people to listen ...
7. It is impossible for scientists to know ...

PRACTICE 18, p. 217

1. c. to
   d. for
   e. to
   f. to
   g. for

2. a. to
   b. for
   c. for
   d. to
   e. to
   f. for
   g. to

PRACTICE 19, p. 217

3. for
4. to
5. for
6. to
7. to

8. for
9. to
10. for
11. for

PRACTICE 20, p. 217

2. goes to the laundromat (in order) to wash his clothes.
3. runs (in order) to get to class on time.
4. open the bedroom windows (in order) to let in some fresh air.
5. calls his parents (in order) to ask them for some money.
6. go back to my hometown (in order) to visit friends and family.
7. go to the library (in order) to study in peace and quiet.

PRACTICE 21, p. 218

2. a. tall enough
   b. too short
3. a. enough money
   b. too poor
4. a. too hot
   b. cool enough

5. a. too sick
   b. well enough
6. a. isn't old enough
   b. is too young

PRACTICE 22, p. 218

3. Ø ... enough
4. too ... Ø
5. too ... Ø
6. Ø ... enough
7. too ... Ø
8. Ø ... enough

PRACTICE 23, p. 219

1. being
2. to spend
3. being
4. being
5. to find
6. being
7. to talk / talking

8. sitting
9. thinking
10. to think
11. speaking
12. making
13. to discuss

PRACTICE 24, p. 219

2. The Johnsons are considering **selling** their antique store.
3. Sam finally finished **building** his vacation home in the mountains.

4. My wife and I **go dancing** at the community center every Saturday night.
5. Suddenly, it began **to rain** and the wind started to blow.
6. The baby is afraid **of being** away from her mother for any length of time.
7. I am excited **about starting** college this September.
8. You can send your application by email.
9. My country is **very** beautiful.
10. **It** is exciting to drive a sports car.
11. My grandparents enjoy **traveling** across the country in a motor home.
12. Elena made this sweater **by hand**.
13. Running it is one of the sports we can participate in at school.
14. **Swimming** with a group of people is more enjoyable than swimming alone.
15. Meeting new people **is** interesting.

PRACTICE 25, p. 220

2. writing
3. to be
4. B: flying
   A: crashing
5. A: arguing … to disagree
   B: raising … to yell
   A: to get
6. A: doing
   B: going shopping
   A: shopping
7. A: putting
   B: forgetting to send
8. A: to have
   B: to learn

PRACTICE 26, p. 221

Down

2. with
4. too
5. picking
6. shopping
9. get
10. sailing
11. by
12. play
13. enough

Across

1. changing
3. moving
7. graduate
8. studying

CHAPTER 14: NOUN CLAUSES

PRACTICE 1, p. 222

A: Do you know who that man is?
B: Yes. I don't know his name, but I know that he's our new grammar teacher.
A: Really? What happened to Ms. Clarkson, our other teacher? I love her class.
B: She's moving to Alaska.
A: Do you know why she's moving to Alaska?
B: I'm not sure. I know that her husband works in the oil industry. Maybe he got a job in Alaska.
A: I'll really miss her. I want to say goodbye before she leaves. Do you know if she's still here?
B: Yes, she is. I saw her in her office about an hour ago.
A: Great! I'm going to run to there now and see her.
B: Okay, but you should hurry. Class starts in ten minutes, and this is our first day with the new teacher. You know how important first impressions are.

PRACTICE 2, p. 222

3. why Sofia left. noun clause
4. ? question
5. ? question
6. when Oliver left. noun clause
7. ? question
8. what calm means. noun clause
9. how long the earth has existed. noun clause
10. ? question
11. ? question
12. where Patagonia is. noun clause

PRACTICE 3, p. 223

2. Adam said
3. we are doing this
4. the new semester starts
5. everyone went
6. the gym is open
7. believes that story
8. phone is ringing

PRACTICE 4, p. 223

3. Henri dropped?
4. her phone number is?
5. keys these are.
6. Clara met?
7. Carlo is absent.
8. it is?
9. Sam is studying?
10. sent Amy flowers?
11. Ms. Gray will call?
12. the president is going to say.
13. is in that room?
14. is in that drawer?
15. a 3D printer costs?

PRACTICE 5, p. 224

2. did he say? … what he said.
3. is the post office? … where the post office is?
4. is it? … what time it is?
5. did David arrive? … when David arrived.
6. is Ana from? … what country Ana is from.
7. was Kathy … why Kathy was …
8. lives … who lives …
9. car is … whose car is …
10. books are these? … whose books these are?

PRACTICE 6, p. 225

2. who lives
3. what he said
4. what kind of car Pat has
5. how old their kids are
6. why you said
7. where I can catch
8. what this word means

PRACTICE 7, p. 225

1. a, a
2. a, b
3. b, a
4. b, a
5. a, b
6. a, b

PRACTICE 8, p. 226

1. people are saying … all the buildings are … my classes start … I register … I am taking … my professors will be
2. it will take … I came … I am

PRACTICE 9, p. 226

2. if / whether Jin has finished medical school yet
3. if / whether Daniel has any time off soon
4. if / whether the flight is on time
5. if / whether there is enough gas in the car
6. if / whether Yuki is married
7. if / whether the Nelsons are going to move
8. if / whether Khaled changed jobs

PRACTICE 10, p. 227

2. gets
3. like
4. runs
5. run
6. takes
7. enjoy
8. seems

PRACTICE 11, p. 227

2. what I'm going to order
3. if / whether there will be
4. where birds go
5. if / whether you can borrow
6. if / whether Nasser has already left
7. why Harold left

PRACTICE 12, p. 228

1. c
2. f
3. a
4. g
5. h
6. b
7. d
8. e

PRACTICE 13, p. 228

2. I predict that …
3. I'm surprised that …
4. Are you certain that …
5. Did you notice that …
6. It's a fact that …
7. A: How do you know that …
   A: I'm still worried that …
8: A: I heard that …
   A: Some people assume that … I think that …

PRACTICE 14, p. 229

2. were worried that Po had been injured
   they were happy when Po called
3. was afraid that he had failed
   was not surprised that he had done well
4. was angry that Mark lied to her
   is sorry that she lent him money
5. that exercise can be good for the heart
   that eating a lot of red meat is bad for the heart

PRACTICE 15, p. 229

2. that the library is open on Sunday
3. that Ann speaks Spanish
4. that Alex passed his French course
5. that Mr. Kozari is going to be at the meeting
6. that these pants are clean

PRACTICE 16, p. 230

1. Alex asked, "Do you smell smoke?"
2. "Something is burning," he said.
3. He asked, "Do you smell smoke? Something is burning."
4. "Do you smell smoke?" he asked. "Something is burning."
5. Rachel said, "The game starts at seven."
6. "The game starts at seven. We should leave here at six," she said.
7. She said, "The game starts at seven. We should leave here at six. Can you be ready to leave then?"

PRACTICE 17, p. 230

One day my friend Laura and I were sitting in her apartment. We were having a cup of tea together and talking about the terrible earthquake that had just occurred in Iran. Laura asked me, "Have you ever been in an earthquake?"

"Yes, I have," I replied.

"Was it a big earthquake?" she asked.

"I've been in several earthquakes, and they've all been small ones," I answered. "Have you ever been in an earthquake?"

"There was an earthquake in my village five years ago," Laura said. "I was in my house. Suddenly the ground started shaking. I grabbed my little brother and ran outside. Everything was moving. I was scared to death. And then suddenly it was over."

"I'm glad you and your brother weren't hurt," I said.

"Yes, we were very lucky. Has everyone in the world felt an earthquake sometime in their lives?" Laura wondered. "Do earthquakes occur everywhere on the earth?"

"Those are interesting questions," I said, "but I don't know the answers."

PRACTICE 18, p. 230

2. his … them
3. she … her
4. him … them
5. they … me … they
6. she … her
7. they … my
8. he … us … they … his

PRACTICE 19, p. 231

	Formal	Informal
2.	was going to be	is going to be
3.	had	has
4.	needed	needs
5.	had flown	has flown
6.	were planning	are planning
7.	didn't want	doesn't want
8.	could take care of	can take care of

PRACTICE 20, p. 232

2. (that) you hadn't found
3. (that) the Smiths had canceled
4. (that) it wouldn't rain
5. (that) the Whites had gotten
6. (that) Mei didn't exercise
7. (that) your computer wasn't working
8. (that) Ali was coming

PRACTICE 21, p. 232

3. if she had
4. if he had changed his
5. how long I had been
6. if she could speak
7. if he would be in his office
8. why she was laughing
9. if I had ever considered

PRACTICE 22, p. 233

2. "Will you be at the meeting?"
3. "Are you going to quit your job?"
4. "Where is your car?"
5. "What did you do after class yesterday?"
6. "Do you know Italian?"
7. "Can you pick up my daughter at school?"
8. "Why aren't you working at your desk?"

PRACTICE 23, p. 233

2. if I had met many people
3. what I was going to study
4. how long I would stay

5. how I liked it here
6. where I was from
7. if the local people were friendly to me
8. how I had chosen this school
9. if I liked the weather here

PRACTICE 24, p. 234
2. (that) he had to talk to her
3. (that) she could meet me
4. (that) she wrote / had written him
5. she would see him
6. what he was doing

PRACTICE 25, p. 234
2. , "You should take careful notes this week to study for the exam."
3. , "I will be absent tomorrow."
4. , "I have a doctor's appointment."
5. , "I'm worried about missing the lecture."
6. , "Could I borrow your notes from class?"
7. , "I have to be absent tomorrow too."
8. , "I'm going to send you both a copy of my notes tomorrow."

PRACTICE 26, p. 235
3. asked
4. told
5. said
6. told … said
7. asked … told … said
8. told … told
9. told
10. asked … said … asked … told

PRACTICE 27, p. 235
2. asked me if / whether I lived
3. told him / replied / said that I had
4. told me / said that he was looking
5. told me / said that he didn't like living
6. asked him if / whether he wanted to move in with me.
7. asked me where my apartment was.
8. replied / told him / said that I lived
9. told me / said that he couldn't move
10. told me / said that he would cancel his
11. asked me if / whether that was okay.
12. told him / replied / said that I was looking forward to having him

PRACTICE 28, p. 236
2. a, b, c, d
3. b, f
4. a, d
5. a, c, e

PRACTICE 29, p. 237
2. what he was doing … where he was going
3. that he was carrying food to the nest
4. why he was working so hard in the beautiful summer weather
5. that if he brought food to the nest in the summer, he could have food in the winter
6. if he could take a break then, and play with him instead of working
7. that he couldn't

8. that if he didn't bring food to the nests in the summer, he wouldn't have any food for the winter
9. that he wasn't worried about the winter because he had plenty of food
10. if those ants ever had any fun
11. that the ants were smart because they had prepared for the winter
12. that it was always a good idea to prepare for the future

PRACTICE 30, p. 238
1. Excuse me. May I ask how old you are?
2. I wonder **if** Rashed **picked up** something for dinner.
3. I'm unsure what Lawrence **does** for a living.
4. Fernando said, "**The** best time for me to meet would be Thursday morning."
5. Eriko asked me if I was coming to the graduation party. I **told** her that I wasn't.
6. I hope that I will do well on my final exams.
7. I'm not sure if the price includes the sales tax or not.
8. My mother asked me, "How many hours did you spend on your homework?"
9. I **asked** my brother, "Are you going to marry Paula?"
10. I'd like to know how you do that.
11. My parents knew what Sam and I **did**.
12. **It is** a fact that unexpected things happen in everyone's lives.

PRACTICE 31, p. 239
1. Wondered
2. Inquired
3. Replied
4. Told
5. Asked
6. Said
7. Answered

APPENDIX 1: PHRASAL VERBS

PRACTICE 1, p. 240
1. out
2. in
3. out
4. up
5. up
6. up
7. down
8. off
9. on
10. off
11. away
12. out
13. off
14. on
15. up
16. down

PRACTICE 2, p. 241
1. off, on
2. up
3. up, down
4. off
5. down, up
6. up
7. up, off
8. out
9. out, out

PRACTICE 3, p. 241
2. my coat, my wedding ring
3. his shoes
4. a story, a fairy tale, an excuse
5. some rotten food, an old shirt
6. a doctor's appointment, a meeting, a trip
7. a puzzle, a math problem
8. a report, some late homework
9. a message, a phone number
10. a box, a sack of mail
11. the light, the computer, the car engine

PRACTICE 4, p. 242

1. on
2. from
3. over
4. off
5. on
6. in/into
7. out of
8. into
9. into

PRACTICE 5, p. 242

1. on
2. over
3. off, on
4. in, out of
5. on, off
6. into
7. into
8. from

PRACTICE 6, p. 242

2. c
3. a
4. g
5. f
6. d
7. e

PRACTICE 7, p. 243

1. out
2. back
3. off
4. up
5. back
6. up
7. back
8. away
9. back
10. out
11. off
12. on
13. down
14. up

PRACTICE 8, p. 244

1. back
2. down
3. out
4. away
5. on
6. up
7. back
8. up
9. back
10. off
11. out, up, off, back

PRACTICE 9, p. 244

3a. into
3b. X
4a. X
4b. into
5a. up
5b. up
6a. away
6b. away
7a. down
7b. X
8a. X
8b. up
9a. away
9b. X
10a. up
10b. up
11a. off
11b. X
12a. from
12b. X

PRACTICE 10, p. 245

1. out
2. in
3. out
4. up
5. out
6. on
7. over
8. out
9. out
10. down
11. out of
12. up
13. around / back
14. over

PRACTICE 11, p. 246

2. out
3. in
4. out
5. out
6. down
7. around
8. out
9. up
10. out
11. out
12. up
13. over

PRACTICE 12, p. 246

1b. on
1c. down
1d. away
1e. out
1f. up
2a. in
2b. out
3a. over
3b. off
3c. on
3d. in
3e. out of
4a. out
4b. up
4c. down
5a. into
5b. up
5c. over
6a. up
6b. off
6c. back
7a. off
7b. back
7c. up
7d. over
8a. in
8b. out
8c. up
8d. up

PRACTICE 13, p. 248

1. out
2. back
3. up
4. up
5. up
6. away
7. out
8. off
9. on
10. back
11. out
12. over
13. over
14. out

PRACTICE 14, p. 248

1. on
2. up
3. out, over
4. out
5. away, out
6. out, up
7. off
8. back
9. up
10. on
11. up
12. over
13. up
14. away
15. out
16. away/back

PRACTICE 15, p. 249

1. down
2. out
3. up
4. in
5. up
6. out
7. down
8. up
9. up
10. on
11. out
12. up
13. in
14. out
15. up
16. back
17. down
18. up
19. up
20. over
21. up
22. off

PRACTICE 16, p. 250

1. off
2. up
3. over
4. down
5. down
6. up
7. out
8. down
9. up
10. up
11. on
12. in, down

PRACTICE 17, p. 250

1b. up
1c. up
1d. out
1e. out
1f. out of
2a. up
2b. up
2c. up
2d. up
2e. into
2f. up

PRACTICE 18, p. 251

1. in on
2. out of
3. along with
4. back from
5. through with
6. up in
7. out for
8. out of
9. up for
10. out for

PRACTICE 19, p. 251

1. out, out for
2. up
3. up for
4. out of
5. back from
6. out of
7. out for
8. through with
9. in on
10. along with

PRACTICE 20, p. 252

2. their neighbors
3. paint
4. rocks
5. assignment
6. Mexico
7. the hospital
8. snakes

PRACTICE 21, p. 252

1. along with
2. over
3. out of
4. out about
5. together
6. back to
7. over to
8. over to
9. around
10. out with
11. away from
12. out for
13. around

PRACTICE 22, p. 253

2. out for
3. back to
4. out with
5. away from
6. along with
7. out to
8. out of
9. over to, in, with

PRACTICE 23, p. 253

2. out
3. back
4. together
5. over to

APPENDIX 2: PREPOSITION COMBINATIONS

PRACTICE 2, p. 255

2. f
3. j
4. e
5. c
6. i
7. a
8. h
9. d
10. g

PRACTICE 3, p. 255

1. to
2. to
3. to
4. with
5. for
6. about
7. of
8. about
9. from
10. with
11. about
12. of

PRACTICE 5, p. 256

1. from
2. with
3. to
4. at
5. in
6. at
7. for
8. with, about

9. with
10. for
11. for

PRACTICE 6, p. 256

1. to
2. from, for
3. to, at
4. to
5. of
6. for
7. with
8. for

PRACTICE 8, p. 257

1. to
2. for
3. for
4. of
5. for, for
6. for
7. to, from
8. to
9. about, in
10. about

PRACTICE 9, p. 258

1a. of
1b. for
1c. of
1d. with
1e. with
1f. of
1g. in
1h. to
2a. about
2b. about
2c. of
2d. of
2e. about
2f. for

PRACTICE 11, p. 259

1. for
2. from
3. for
4. on
5. with
6. in
7. at
8. to
9. with
10. of
11. to
12. to, about
13. with, about
14. to, about

PRACTICE 12, p. 259

1. about
2. from
3. of
4. to
5. to
6. from
7. with
8. with
9. for, at
10. with, about, to, to, about

PRACTICE 14, p. 260

1. with
2. to
3. from
4. about
5. to
6. about/of
7. at
8. for
9. for
10. for
11. about
12. to
13. about
14. like
15. for
16. at

PRACTICE 15, p. 261

1. g
2. i
3. c
4. j
5. b
6. h
7. a
8. f
9. e
10. d

PRACTICE 17, p. 262

1. to, for
2. for
3. of
4. for
5. on
6. for

7. on
8. to
9. from
10. on
11. of

12. of
13. to
14. from
15. from

PRACTICE 18, p. 262

3a. C
3b. C
4a. I
4b. C
5a. C
5b. C

6a. C
6b. C
7a. C
7b. I
8a. I
8b. C

PRACTICE 20, p. 263

1. on
2. from

3. about
4. for

5. about
6. from
7. to, about
8. to
9. by

10. from
11. by
12. to
13. about
14. from

PRACTICE 21, p. 264

1. on
2. about
3. with
4. from
5. from
6. to, for
7. of
8. to

9. to
10. to
11. for
12. from
13. on
14. on
15. of
16. about

NOTES